Jackets
TAILORING MADE EASY!
FOR Real People

**MARTA ALTO,
SUSAN NEALL,
AND PATI PALMER**

Fourth revised expanded edition of
Easy, Easier, Easiest, Tailoring

Designed by Linda Wisner
Photography by Pati Palmer
Technical Illustrations by Kate Pryka
Fashion Illustrations by Diane Russell
Styling and Sewing by Marta Alto
Cover by Linda Wisner and Pati Palmer
Technical and Copy Editing by Ann Gosch

Palmer/Pletsch

Aussie Dictionary

Since one of the authors lives and teaches in Sydney, Australia, and since our books are sold in Australia, we need to clarify meanings of American English terms for our Australian friends.

American English	Australian English
Dress form	Dressmaker's model
Right sides together	Right sides facing
Muslin	Calico
Quilter's cotton	Homespun
Lapel	Revere
Center	Centre
Frogs/loop closures	Rouleaux loops
Sergers	Overlockers
Notions	Haberdashery
Closet	Wardrobe
Catch Stitch	Herringbone Stitch
Slip Stitch	Ladder Stitch

Acknowledgements

There are many people to thank over the years for their contribution to our own education in tailoring, such as our mothers, our college professors, our previous employers, our talented staff that traveled teaching Palmer/Pletsch seminars all over the world for 20-plus years, Vogue and McCall Pattern company staffs, and you, our students, many of whom gave us input on this book.

Marta would also like to thank Bev Smith, author of a book on custom tailoring for men. Marta took classes from Bev in the '70s and learned many of the techniques that she would build upon over the years and adapt to women's tailoring.

Also, thanks to Pati's daughter Melissa Watson for being the "novice" sewer who read the book while making her first blazer—in velveteen.

And, as when any major project is completed, we all must thank the patience of our families including Jerry Alto, Phillip Neall, and Paul Tucker.

Several of our students and teachers offered to read the manuscript for clarity and contributed as technical and copy editors. They include the following: Rachael Carlson, Connie Hamilton, Mary McCarthy, Janet Dapson, Sandy Hagness, Colleen Mikkelson, Tara Hendison, Nancy Seifert, Meryl Wynne, Janice Aston, and Laura Hefferan

A very special thank you to our talented and persistent design director Linda Wisner who tirelessly worked into the night to meet our press deadline. It is amazing to watch her work her magic on rough pages and turn them into design masterpieces. Also, to Jeff Watson for running the company while Pati wrote. And a special thanks to Marta Alto for sewing all of those clothes used in photography as well as being a writer and editor.

Cover photo:

Marta Alto, co-author, in silk suiting. *You can read more about Marta on the facing page.*

Anastasia Alto in embossed velvet. *Anastasia has grown up with sewing and now teaches her friends. She is enrolled in Oregon State University's Geriatric Counseling program in Bend, Oregon.*

Laurie Harsh in Pago's Santa Cruise. *Laurie owns The FabricShop Network, a trade association for independent fabric and quilt retailers (www.fabshopnet.com). The association provides online resource information and sponsors promotional events for consumers at www.fabshophop.com.*

The original book, *Easy, Easier, Easiest Tailoring* by Pati Palmer and Susan Pletsch was written in 1977, updated in 1995, and in 2000 when the 26th printing occurred. Nearly 300,000 copies have been sold. (It is still in print for those wanting alternative tailoring techniques.)

Jackets for Real People is the fourth, expanded edition, copyright © 2006 by by Marta Alto, Susan Neall, and Pati Palmer.

Library of Congress Control Number: 2006900424
Published by Palmer/Pletsch Inc., 1801 N.W. Upshur Street, Suite 100, Portland, OR 97209, U.S.A.
Printed by Quebecor World, USA   Second printing September 2009
ISBN 978-0-935278-66-8

ABOUT THE AUTHORS

Marta Alto

Marta's career as a sewing expert began during her summer "vacations" from studying at Oregon State University, when she sewed costumes at the Oregon Shakespeare Festival in Ashland. That led to a job at San Francisco State University teaching drama students how to sew costumes. As a result, Marta learned how to sew without patterns and to fit many actors' figures.

Marta's unconventional problem-solving approach to fit and sewing techniques grew out of this experience. Pati used to cringe at Marta's less-than-technically-correct solutions, but now enjoys Marta's creative problem solving.

After five years in San Francisco, Marta returned to Oregon in 1972 with her 4-year-old son and became a custom dressmaker at a major Oregon department store. She sewed designer clothing for mothers of brides who wanted a special dress that fitted and for people wanting outfits out of that wonderful "new" fabric, Ultrasuede. Marta then became assistant manager, then manager of the store's sewing school where she taught both custom and speed tailoring. After the birth of her second child in 1977, she "retired" to teaching sewing in Portland, then Seattle. In 1981, Marta joined Palmer/Pletsch and traveled throughout the United States, Canada, and Australia teaching Ultrasuede, fit, tailoring and serger seminars.

In 1986, Marta became a Palmer/Pletsch corporate workshop educator. She is also co-author of *Fit for REAL People, Pants for REAL People , The Serger Idea Book, Sewing Ultrasuede,* and is the talent in most Palmer/Pletsch videos and DVDs. She also helped develop the Palmer/Pletsch interfacing line. She currently teaches a number of sewing topics at the Palmer/Pletsch School of Sewing in Portland, OR, and does writing and research on sewing trends.

Susan Neall

Sue's lifelong passion for sewing started from the cradle. With a mother who was a pattern maker and grader and three equally gifted aunts, all involved in Australia's growing fashion manufacturing industry, Sue was sewing before she went to school. She has never stopped.

After completing four years of fashion teaching at the Fashion School at East Sydney Technical College, Sue taught in New South Wales for several years before making a career-changing move to become the national education manager for the McCall Pattern Company. The shift from government education to home-sewing industry and the long term friendships made at McCall's have influenced and directed her 25 years of writing, promoting, and teaching throughout Australia.

Also, during her career in the fashion sewing and craft industry Sue has worked as Bernina Sewing Machines national sewing promoter, executive director of The Australian Sewing and Craft Industry Association (ASCIA), co-founder of the Australian Sewing Guild, craft consultant *Better Homes & Gardens* magazine and T.V., craft editor Parents & Children Magazine, sewing and craft writer for *Family Circle* Magazine. She also started *Australian Stitches* magazine.

Sue is presently working as director of Palmer/Pletsch Education, Australia; editor *Australian Stitches* magazine; fashion sewing presenter for the Australian Stitches and Craft Shows; and sewing presenter Today Extra NBN Television.

In between meeting Pati Palmer for the first time in 1983 and joining Palmer/Pletsch in 1996, Sue and her long time best friend/husband, Phillip, took a little time out to have their three children, Ben, Katie and Rebecca.

Pati Palmer

Pati Palmer has been teaching sewing for over 30 years. She conducted seminars throughout North America and Australia for 15 years, traveling 26 weeks per year, before establishing the Palmer/Pletsch International School of Sewing in Portland where she now trains consumers and sewing educators. She is the author of 10 sewing books, editor/publisher of 20 more books and 11 how-to videos, and creator of eight Palmer/Pletsch sewing notion products. From 1980 to the present, Pati has designed and written instructions for more than 100 patterns for The McCall Pattern Co. Prior to that she designed for Vogue. She is currently consulting with Unique Pattern Co. of Halifax, N.S, Canada, in hopes of perfecting its system of fitting sewing patterns using body scanning and computer-aided custom-fit designs.

Pati has appeared with Regis Philbin and on "Good Morning Australia," and has had her books and patterns featured in *Family Circle, Vogue,* **Australian Stitches**, and all of the major sewing publications. She was national chairman of the Business Section of the American Association of Family and Consumer Sciences, a co-founder of the Consumer Science Business Professionals (now the Consumer Trends Forum), and advisor to the founders of the national Professional Association of Custom Clothiers. She was also voted entrepreneur of the year by the Business Section of the American Association of Family and Consumer Sciences. Pati holds a B.S. degree in Clothing, Textiles and Related Arts from Oregon State University. Her daughter Melissa Watson, who many remember growing up, is now in college.

Students come from around the world for one-week "Sewing Vacations" at her sewing school in Portland. She also trains teachers in the Palmer/Pletsch methods.

Table of Contents

The Four Blocks of Time

Many people do not feel they have time to make a jacket. And most people don't have an entire day to devote to sewing.

The secret to sewing is dividing the process into self-motivating blocks of time. This is reprinted from our book *Mother Pletsch's Painless Sewing*.

First Block

PLANNING AND FITTING
(25% of total sewing time!)
In this block, fit your pattern and collect everything you'll need to sew this garment.

STOP!

Second Block

CUTTING, MARKING, APPLYING INTERFACING, AND PINNING THE PIECES INTO A READY-TO-FIT POSITION

Don't stop after cutting. It's much easier to apply interfacing while all the pieces are flat. Then pin all seams together for a quick fit check. Fit. Then repin seams for sewing.
STOP!!
Next time you sew, it will be easy. Even at 5 a.m. we can sew a seam. No thinking is required.

Third Block

SEW AND PRESS
This could be more than one session. The point here is to **prepare** for the finishing before quitting. Have you ever sewn a garment that is still waiting for a hem? Before the "sewing" segment is finished, pin up the hem, gather the buttons, thread, needle, scissors, and pincushion and put them into a plastic bag. Attach the bag to the hanger with the jacket on it.

Now you can quit!

Fourth Block

FINISHING
Now you are ready for TV or telephone work! Take hand sewing along on a trip or a visit with friends.

CHAPTER 1
About Sewing Jackets

1977 edition   1983 edition   1995 edition

A Little History

Constructing jackets was once done entirely by hand, using special interfacing and stitches to give permanent shape to a garment. The interfacing was a woven wool blended with goat hair fibers. This hair canvas was bulky, so darts were often cut out and the raw edges butted together and stitched onto seam tape to hold them in place. Even the seam allowances were removed and a lightweight tape was fell-stitched to the edges of the canvas and to the fabric stitching line.

You could mold the wool into the shape you wanted using steam, and then the goat hair would hold the shape, like pins in a pincushion.

In the 1950s, Edna Bryte Bishop studied manufacturing methods and taught ways to sew tailored jackets by machine. In 1959, Marjorie Arch wrote the book *The Bishop Method of Clothing Construction*. Pati took tailoring in Montana in 1965 from Emma Briscoe who taught the factory Bishop Method. Interfacing was stitched to the undercollar by machine. (She remembers wanting to use one of the new bonded wools and her teacher reluctantly allowing her the experience.)

When Pati graduated from Oregon State University in 1968, she became an educator for the Armo interfacing company the same year it introduced the first FUSIBLE hair canvas, Acro. The Armo educational representatives taught both custom tailoring and several easier methods such as sewing hair canvas to an underlining by machine, fusing it to an underlining, or fusing directly to the fashion fabric. Jackets ended up pretty rigid.

Today's fusibles are much softer and higher performance than those of the 1960s. In the 1990s, Armani used these new weft fusibles to create a softer style jacket—and the rest is history. In 2000, Pati and Marta developed their own line of these weft fusible interfacings for the home sewer. (See chapter 4.)

Pati Palmer and Susan Pletsch wrote one of the first speed tailoring books in 1977. *Easy, Easier, Easiest Tailoring* was a great tailoring reference for a variety of techniques. It was revised in 1983 and again in 1995.

The Famous 8-hour Blazer

After designing for Vogue Patterns from 1975 to 1980, Pati and Susan switched to McCall's. They designed the 8-hour blazer that was featured in *Family Circle* magazine with a circulation of seven million. About this time, John Molloy's book *The Woman's Dress for Success Book* advised business women to wear suits to compete with men. The blazer pattern sold 60,000 units its third week on sale, and a million the first year. Timing is everything!

That same year, Palmer/Pletsch educators, including co-author Marta Alto, as well as writer Barbara Weiland, Karen Dillon, Lynn Raasch, and Susan Pletsch, taught over 900 seminars throughout North America.

We love this article from the *Vancouver (BC) Sun*. Well, at least it didn't take 85 hours to make a jacket!

It took 11 hours to make 8-hour blazer

7

These seminar ads appeared in the early '80s.

In this book, we are going to teach you only the newest, easiest jacket techniques. WHY? Because they work! However, so you will gain an appreciation of what YOU missed from the past or, in case you want to custom tailor, we will describe hand stitches used in custom tailoring, some of which are occasionally used even with today's faster methods.

What Makes It Tailored?

"Tailoring" is a method of sewing that makes a garment more durable than traditional dressmaking. It generally applies to coats and jackets. "Tailored" can also refer to a "man-tailored" fashion look with crisp details, masculine fabrics, and men's suit styling.

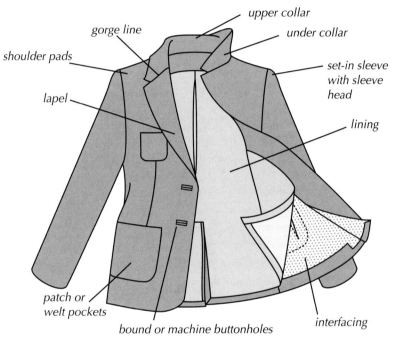

A blazer, which we define as a jacket that has a lapel, rolled collar, and a straight, uncuffed sleeve, contains virtually all of the traditional techniques that set tailoring apart from dressmaking.

THE TERMS

A lapel-style jacket has special terms you may not have seen before: collar stand, collar fall, lapel, roll line on collar and lapel, and a gorge line (where the collar and lapel are joined).

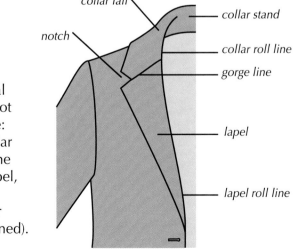

Custom Tailoring Methods

These specialty stitches had a place in custom tailoring. Many have been replaced by using quality fusible interfacings, yet you might need them on occasion.

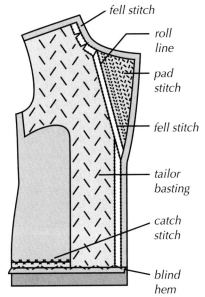

- fell stitch
- roll line
- pad stitch
- fell stitch
- tailor basting
- catch stitch
- blind hem

Pad stitch - small stitch that attaches interfacing to under collar and lapel. It adds body and if done over the curve of your hand, creates a permanently rolled collar and lapel.

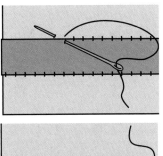

Tailor basting - large pad stitches used to hold large areas of interfacing to fashion fabric on a jacket front. Use a small needle so you catch only a fiber of fashion fabric so the stitches won't show.

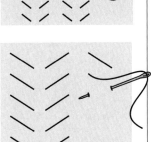

Fell stitch - a 3/8" (1cm) long stitch used to hold tape firmly in place.

Catch stitch - a loose stitch used to catch edges of hem interfacing in place. Also, it is currently used to temporarily keep welts together in double-welt pockets.

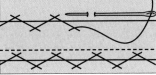

Stab Stitch - a loose running stitch that joins two seams that fall on top of each other. Needle goes into well of the seam on top at an angle and comes out of well on the under layer. It is used to attach the upper collar/facing seam to the under collar/jacket seam.

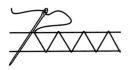

Blind hem - a loose stitch between the layers that makes a **truly** invisible hem. Use a size 10 sharp needle and catch only a fiber of your fabric. Make each stitch about 3/8" apart. (1cm)

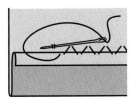

Slip stitch - used for jump hem in lining and to attach patch pockets. The needle goes through the fold, so when the thread is pulled tight, the stitches disappear.

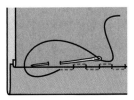

Today's Easier Tailoring Methods

Many talented seamstresses balk at the thought of making a jacket. They think that it's just too hard! Well, think again. Marta is a super speedy seamstress who can make a jacket in 8 hours—but Susan (who usually sews at a snail's pace) can now make that 8-hour jacket too. It is as easy as 1,2,3! If you make the same jacket more than once, but in different fabrics, you can fine-tune your skills. Each time it will go together faster, because you won't have to read ALL the steps.

Today's fusible interfacings are non-bulky, so can be caught in seams, eliminating the need to fell stitch tape to the edges. Fusibles stabilize, eliminating stretch in bias areas such as the roll line. They have a thermoplastic coating, so they can be fused flat, then reheated to create a roll in the lapel and collar, eliminating the need for pad stitching over your hand. Hems are interfaced with fusibles, so catch stitching a hair canvas in a hemline is not necessary.

Remember, all of the processes required to make a jacket are simply extensions of dressmaking, so drop the dreaded "tailoring" word and just follow the FIVE Palmer/Pletsch "Ps" on the next page to make quick and easy jackets today's way. These "Ps" will make sewing great-looking jackets easier!

Palmer/Pletsch's Five "Ps"

1. **Personal pattern and fabric selection.**
   For your first tailoring project, use a simple pattern style such as a cardigan. (See page 12 for easy style and detail suggestions.) Use a no-fail, easy-to-tailor fabric. (See page 15.)

2. **Patient fitting with no-fear altering.**
   Tissue-fit your pattern first. (See page 34.)

3. **Perfect preparation, cutting, marking, and interfacing.** Use fusible interfacings—now easy and good quality. (See page 55.)

4. **Precision stitching** using the fastest methods.

5. **Purposeful pressing**—the difference between handmade and homemade. (See page 29.)

Why Learn Tailoring Techniques?

1. You will improve all your sewing skills by learning tailoring techniques. Special tailoring techniques can also be used for super effects in sewing many other garments. For example, the taping technique taught on page 65 can be used to prevent "gaposis" on the V-neck of a daring evening dress. You will master trimming, grading and pressing, as well as great collar points. All your future sewing will seem easier.

2. Making your own tailored garments is the only way to guarantee a perfect fit, and when your jacket fits, it will be the most comfortable and flattering piece in your closet. The ultimate jacket fit test is being able to wear your jacket comfortably all day, buttoned (without gaposis), and leaving it on for the drive home.

3. You can make your sewing time as profitable as possible by making only those things you can't afford to buy. Susan says she can afford $20 T-shirts but refuses to spend $1200 for the quality jacket she loves. She multiplies the cost of the jacket "ingredients" by seven to come up with the approximate cost of a comparable ready-to-wear garment. When you use $50-$200 worth of ingredients, your jacket will compare to a $350-$1400 designer jacket—a potential savings of $1200! Tailoring can save tons of money.

4. Individuality! As with all your fashion sewing, making your own tailored garments is the only way to have the perfect style, in the perfect fabric, in the perfect color. Sew for your unique body, personality and lifestyle.

5. We will cover tailoring with fusible interfacings. The information applies to many jacket and coat styles.

6. Because fashion constantly changes, learning to tailor will prepare you to sew any new fashion look. For example, bound buttonholes go in and out of fashion.

Optimize Time—Sew an Outfit!!

Spend more time, but get better value from your time spent. Don't just make a jacket or coat—make an outfit!

Make a top and a bottom out of two coordinating fabrics and you will have as many as 16 ways to wear your new pieces.

If you are making a skirt or pant to go with your jacket, sew one of those simpler pieces first to get used to sewing your fabric. If you make a pant and a jacket, you will often have enough fabric for a FREE vest—a real bonus!

You will also be able to wear the same accessories with your coordinating fabrics, saving shopping time and money.

Capsule wardrobe from the Palmer/Pletsch book Looking Good *by Nancy Nix-Rice. See this book for more great wardrobe ideas.*

CHAPTER 2

Pattern Selection

Select a Pattern with Good Lines for YOU

If you are not sure of the best lines for you, try on ready-to-wear or analyze the lines of your favorite clothes. Remember, almost any style or length of jacket will add height and be slenderizing if the jacket and pants or skirt are in the same color fabric.

NOTE: ALWAYS look at the line drawings on the pattern or in the pattern book as they will give you the true shape of the fashion.

Looks that tend to broaden the figure:

double-breasted with wide overlap, wide lapels, square bottom

NOTE: 2-button double-breasted jackets with narrow overlaps will not add much width.

Looks that tend to slenderize the figure:

single-breasted, medium width lapels, rounded bottom, and deep "V" lapel (one- or two-button jacket)

short, boxy style

long jacket with princess seaming

Choose an Attractive Jacket Length

If a pant or skirt fits well, the jacket length is not as crucial. As a general rule, jackets should not stop at the fullest part of the hip as this will emphasize hip width. A more flattering length is just above or below the fullest part. Overall proportion must also be considered. A short person may look better in a shorter jacket. Before making a jacket, pin the pattern pieces together and try on with the finished pant or skirt. A full-length mirror will give you your answers.

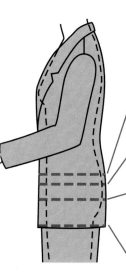

Short jackets—*best with skirts. If worn with pants, must fit well. Best if same color. Excellent for short people.*

Above fullest part of hip—*works well if everything fits well. Excellent for thin or short people.*

Just below fullest part of hip—*a compromise length for fuller hips when fashion decrees shorter jackets. Works with both pants and skirts.*

Well below fullest part of hip—*hides hips. Works well on average to tall people.*

Find a flattering length before you invest in a pattern by "snoop" shopping. Try on ready-made jackets of different length with both skirts and pants. When you find the lengths you like best, take out your trusty purse tape measure and measure the finished back length! Compare to the "finished back length" printed on the pattern envelope. REMEMBER, you can adjust the length of any pattern below the waistline.

Styles
Easiest to Most Difficult

Make life easy, right from the start, by selecting the easiest pattern design for your first jacket. The following styles range from the EASIEST to the most DIFFICULT:

EASIEST

cardigan style without buttons

cardigan style with buttons such as the Chanel style

LESS EASY

shawl collar style

classic blazer

MOST DIFFICULT

zip-front jacket with darts with or without collar

EASY

funnel neckline

MORE DIFFICULT

oversized lapel jacket

double-breasted, peaked-lapel blazer

A coat is just a long jacket and can be made from any of the above styles.

Shapes
Easiest to Most Difficult

The following shapes are from EASIEST to more DIFFICULT:

unshaped

shoulder princess

very fitted

armhole princess

13

Details

Easiest to Most Difficult

The following details range from the EASIEST to the most DIFFICULT:

POCKETS

no pockets

side seam pockets

patch pockets

welt pockets

CLOSURES

1. none
2. buttons with machine buttonholes
3. zippers
4. tie closure
5. hidden placket
6. button and loop
7. buttons with bound buttonholes.

1

2

3

4

5

6

7

SLEEVE DETAILS

cut-on sleeve

one-piece set-in

2-piece set-in

2-piece set-in with vent

set-in with cu

14

CHAPTER 3
Fabrics

Choose an Easy Fabric

Holly Wells, a high school teacher from Provo, Utah, in the photo above selects fabrics for a wardrobe during a Palmer/Pletsch workshop. SEW many choices! Here are some tips for picking jacket fabrics.

The **EASY FABRIC CHART** shows sewability at a glance. If you want to sew an easy jacket, choose fabric from the "Easiest to Sew" column. These fabrics will fuse, sew and press quickly with professional results. Those in the "Not as Fast to Sew" column require more skill and may require fusing an interfacing to an underlining fabric.

A key to fast and easy jackets with fusibles is to choose a medium-weight fabric with surface texture or design. A fabric with lumps and bumps (tweed), fuzz (flannel), texture (linen), or design (herringbone) will camouflage your interfacing and inner construction.

If a fabric doesn't ease well, it will be harder to handle. You will be more likely to get puckers in your set-in sleeves, seams, or collar notches. Tightly woven fabrics, permanent press fabrics,

microfibers, and fabrics with a high percentage of non-absorbent fiber (nylon, polyester) do not ease well. A fabric with all three of these characteristics will be difficult to tailor.

In the photo above the top and bottom curves are the same size. A hem was turned up, eased, and steamed. The hem ease in the top, a wool tweed, disappears after steaming. The ease in the bottom fabric, a poly/cotton, tightly woven, permanent press fabric, will not disappear no matter how much you steam it.

Easy Fabric Chart

Easiest to sew	Not as Fast to Sew
Wool Tweed	Lightweight Cottons
Wool Crepe	Corduroy
Wool Flannel	Wool Coating
Suit-weight Silk	Velveteen
Linen	Microfiber
Wool Blends	Suede Fabrics
Linen-like Fabrics	Dress-Weight Rayon
Stretch Woven	or Silk
Wool Gabardine	Seersucker
Tencel	Velvet
Ultrasuede	Evening Fabrics
Denim	Sportswear Fabrics
Rayon Suiting	

Image Consultant Ethel Harms helps Roberta Joiner from Santa Cruz, California, select a wardrobe based on her color palette.

Sewing and Shaping Tips for Fashion Fabrics

The fabrics discussed here correspond to the chart on the previous page. (The interfacing suggestions are from our PerfectFuse line that is sold in the U.S. and Australia, page 23.)

Wool Tweed - The easiest jacket fabric. It eases well so your sleeves will set in perfectly, and the texture hides inside construction. Some fusibles won't adhere well to lumpy surfaces, so always test fusibles on a sample to see which is best. We suggest PerfectFuse Tailor for the jacket front and under collar. Lightweight tweeds may need PerfectFuse Light on the back, side, and upper collar. A bias strip of fusible interfacing is used in the jacket hem and sleeve hem in pieces without a fusible underlining.

Wool Crepe - Our very favorite fabric for a classic blazer jacket. We find crepe looks wonderful and lasts longer when fused with PerfectFuse Tailor in the jacket front and under collar. Fuse the back, facing, upper collar and side pieces with PerfectFuse Light. It may be necessary to add extra layers in the lapel area of the front and the stand of the under collar. We fuse only the hem area of the sleeve.

Wool Flannel - If you use wool flannel, use a good one. A medium- to heavy-weight 100% wool that is not too tightly woven is easiest to sew. Generally it is necessary to fuse PerfectFuse Tailor to the jacket front and under collar. Use bias strips of PerfectFuse Light on hems elsewhere. If it is a lightweight flannel, treat it like wool crepe above.

Suit-weight silk - The perfect year-round fabric in any climate. Silk tweeds can lose body after wearing and cleaning, so interface them in the same manner as for wool crepe. Some of our students even fuse fitted sleeves to keep the elbow from stretching.

Photo courtesy The McCall Pattern Co.

Linen - Suit-weight 100% linen is one of our favorites for an easy-to-sew jacket. Yes, it wrinkles! However, fusing helps keep wrinkles under control. Fuse PerfectFuse Tailor to the fronts and under collar. You may want PerfectFuse Medium on the upper collar and facing. Use PerfectFuse Light on the back and side pieces. Fusing the sleeves is optional.

Marta Alto wears a linen jacket she machine embroidered. This jacket is loose, "unconstructed," and interfaced in collar and facing only.

Wool Blends - These fabrics are less expensive, sometimes washable, looser in weave and lighter than 100% wool. Polyester, rayon, and nylon are the most common blending fibers. If blends are at least 50% wool, they will still behave like wool and be easy to sew. Treat like wool crepe for fusing jacket pieces.

Linen-like fabrics - Come in all weights from the heavier rayon/polyester blends to lightweights. The heavier, loosely woven fabrics are far easier to sew than the lighter, tightly woven blends. Use PerfectFuse Tailor on the front and the under collar and PerfectFuse Light on the back and side pieces.

Pati wears a poly/rayon/linen blend called Santa Cruz from Pago. It is easy to sew, washable, and looks like silk. She used PerfectFuse Light on the facings and on both upper and under collars in this totally machine-made, unlined jacket.

Wool Gabardine - Made from long wool fibers that are highly twisted. Wool gabardine is tightly woven, has a smooth surface, and is generally lightweight. It is very popular with designers because it wears very well. Because it has a smooth surface, it shows press marks easily and requires careful pressing to avoid an overworked appearance. It is possible to use today's weft insertion fusibles, but always make a test sample to be sure you get a bond. Use PerfectFuse Tailor on the front and under collar. Using PerfectFuse Light on the upper collar and facing helps prevent seam allowance ridges from showing though. Using it on the back and side pieces will help prevent puckers in the seams.

Tencel® - A new rayon-type fabric, often made to mimic linen. The heavier Tencels are more appropriate for sewing jackets. Treat them like linen and linen-like fabrics.

Ultrasuede® - An easy fabric to sew, Ultrasuede works well with fusibles. Use PerfectFuse Medium on the front and under collar. Ultrasuede requires special sewing techniques. (See *Sewing Ultrasuede Brand Fabrics* by Marta Alto, Pati Palmer and Barbara Weiland. In the Ultrasuede video Marta Alto sews a entire jacket..

Denim - Denim is a heavier cotton that works well for many Jacket styles. Preshrink by washing and drying the fabric at least twice before cutting. Use fusible interfacing in the same manner as for linen-like fabrics.

Rayon Suiting - These fabrics come in various weights and textures. Treat them like wool crepe.

Happy students in wool flannel and gabardine after completing a Palmer/Pletsch Tailoring Workshop! Lynn Weddell, Alice Lorenzen, and Nancy Seifert.

Corduroy - This is a cotton fabric that needs to be preshrunk before fusing interfacing. Narrow wales will fuse better than wide-wale. If sewing a blazer style jacket fuse interfacings like wool crepe. For more casual styles, see lightweight cottons.

Wool Coating - Perfect for a coat, which is just a long jacket! Generally you need to fuse PerfectFuse Tailor to the facing and under collar only.

Velveteen -
Cotton velveteen is drycleanable and washable, but it is not as pretty after washing. Press from the wrong side. Needle holes will show if you have let out any seams, especially if they were first pressed. Fuse to the front with PerfectFuse Tailor and to the facings with PerfectFuse Light.

Melissa Watson wanted a very fitted, two-button velveteen blazer even though being advised against it for her FIRST jacket. She forged ahead fearlessly. "I learned a lot reading this book while sewing my jacket. Now I want to try an easier, less bulky fabric...satin!"

Microfiber - Generally polyester, but sometimes rayon, microfibers can look like suede, satin, silk, and other drapey fabrics. Because they are tightly woven and require careful pressing, we prefer to use them for softer jacket styles. Their tight weave makes it difficult to get a firm bond when fusing. Interface the facings and collars with PerfectFuse Sheer, which bonds the best, but let it cool thoroughly before testing the bond. Use "taut sewing" for pucker-free seams. Pull on the fabric in front of and behind the needle evenly while sewing.

Dress-weight Silk and Rayon - Some of these can be tightly woven and need "taut sewing" to keep seams from puckering. Use PerfectFuse Sheer interfacing for best results on these smooth fabrics. If the fabric has texture use PerfectFuse Light interfacing to give body to all the garment pieces for a more structured jacket.

Velvet - Fusible interfacing will cause the nap of these silk or rayon fabrics to flatten. It is best to fuse interfacing to a sew-in underlining like silk organza or cotton batiste. Then attach it to the fabric. See page 26. Press seams by steaming above the velvet lightly and finger press flat.

Anastasia Alto's jacket is from embossed velvet. Marta used craft felt for the undercollar.

Sportswear Fabrics - These tightly woven polyester, poly/cotton, or nylon fabrics are more difficult to sew. They are best for unstructured styles. Use PerfectFuse Sheer on collars and facings.

Suede Fabric, Chamois - These are napped fabrics, generally polyester wovens, and can ravel easily. (However, some are a knit base.) Best for unstructured styles. Use PerfectFuse Sheer interfacing on the collar and facings which will also prevent raveling when you trim closely.

Lightweight Cotton - This is the perfect fabric for a summer jacket, most often left unlined. Generally we interface only the facing and the upper and under collars. The seams will need to be finished with serging or other techniques, when the jacket is unlined. See page 20.

Photo courtesy of McCall Pattern Co.

Seersucker - This fabric has built-in puckers. Don't flatten them with fusibles. Instead, treat like velvet.

Knits -Heavy wool knits and polyester fleece are nice for soft style jackets. Interface the facing only if using buttons.

Evening Wear Fabrics - There are many beautiful fabrics such as brocades, satin, beaded fabrics and laces. The heavier textured fabrics can take tailor weight or medium interfacing. PerfectFuse Sheer will work on beaded and lace or burn out sheers.

Alice Lorenzen, Indianapolis, wears an award-winning embellished evening jacket made from silk shantung.

During a workshop, Marta Alto helps Connie Hunnel with her mother-of-the-bride dress for an evening wedding. The polyester satin with cutwork selvage borders in two widths was hand beaded. Her suit will be stunning.

Organize Your Stash

Catalog your fabrics. Keep swatches in a small notebook, an accordion-fold wallet photo holder, or on index cards. Note the yardage, width, fiber content, care information, and maybe even when and where you bought it and, just for fun, the price. Carry swatches with you when shopping to buy coordinating fabrics......or shoes!

100% linen
5 yards
45"-wide
Cy Rudnicks
1983
Under bed in guest room

Hand Woven
rayon/silk
3 yards
45"-wide
Dry Clean
$30 per yard
Puyallup 2

100% Cotton
Velveteen
2½ yards
$12 per yard
60"-wide
Josephine's
Dry goods
2005
Best to dryclean

Fashion Fabric Care Guide

Read the bolt-end label for fiber and care information.

Washable Fabrics

Preshrink your fabric and linings if you plan to wash the finished garment.

Preshrink in the same manner you would wash:

◆ Don't overcrowd the washing machine.

◆ Use short, cold-water cycles to preserve colors.

◆ Use detergent when preshrinking.

◆ Use a cool rinse with synthetic fibers to minimize wrinkling.

◆ Don't over-dry fabrics or they will pill and fade.

Dry-cleanable Fabrics

Preshrink fabric to be dry-cleaned by having the dry cleaner steam the fabric, or steam it yourself with one of those wonderful "shot-of-steam" type irons.

Slowly and thoroughly steam every inch of the fabric. Allow to cool and dry before moving. (See page 57.)

We find this comparable to the "London shrink" method used in the past.

Seam Finishes

Lined Jackets

These need very little or no seam finishing.

Pinking - If the fabric is ravely, pink the edges with pinking shears. Don't squeeze the sheers while you are cutting or they will chew your fabric. Hold them loosely! Or, use your serger to finish the seams.

Unlined Jackets

Make the inside of your jacket look professional by using one of these easy finishes as you sew the seams:

Turn and stitch - Stitch 1/4" (6mm) from raw edge of the seam allowance. Turn the edge under on that stitching line and edgestitch.

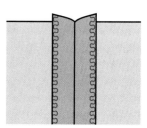

Serged edges - Barely trim the edge of the seam allowance as you overedge with a 2- or 3-thread serged stitch. Marta loves to use a decorative thread like a heavy rayon to finish the seams in unlined jackets.

Hong Kong seam finish - Sew a 1"-wide bias strip of lining fabric to edge of seam, right sides together, 1/4" from edge. Trim to 1/8". Turn bias strip to the wrong side and top-stitch in the well of the seam from the top side to catch it in place. This is the "couture" way to finish unlined jackets.

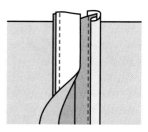

Double-fell Seam - Turn each seam allowance under 1/4" (6mm) and edgestitch along the fold, through all layers. This gives a row of topstitching on each side of the seam-line and totally encases raw edges. This method can make a garment reversible.

Zigzagging - Use this finish for medium and heavyweight fabrics. Use a stitch length of 2mm and width of 3mm.

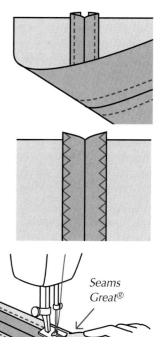

Seams Great® - Wrap the 1/2" (1.3cm) strip of nylon tricot around a seam allowance and start sewing. Pull on the tricot slightly to wrap the edge as you stitch. It is excellent for VERY ravelly fabrics. Avoid a hot iron when pressing seams.

Seams Great®

CHAPTER 4
Shaping Fabrics

Shaping fabrics give body to a garment to make it more durable. This is even more important in jackets. We use much more subtle shaping and easier methods than in years past, but the need for support for your fashion fabric hasn't changed.

THE TERMINOLOGY

Lining - Generally, a slippery fabric that covers the inside construction and allows the garment to slide on and off easily.

Interfacing - Provides shape, body, and support to edges, details and sometimes entire pieces when fusibles are used.

Underlining - A lightweight fabric such as silk organza that provides shape, body, and opacity to large pieces of fabric. It is included in the seams with the fashion fabric.

Interlining (optional) - A lofty layer of fabric stitched to the back of a lining to provide warmth.

NOTE: In the past an **interfacing** was used to add firmness to edges and details, whereas an **underlining** would be placed on the wrong side of an entire garment piece to add body or opacity. Today, in the world of fusible interfacings, we often fuse an interfacing to an entire piece. So, do we call this interfacing an underlining?

We generally refer to it as an interfacing when it is on an edge such as a hem, a detail such as a collar, or the entire front of a jacket.

If we hand-baste silk organza or other light-weight fabric to the wrong side of an entire piece, we call it an underlining. If we fuse to the back side panels, or sleeves, we generally call it a **fused underlining**.

The Critical Issue: Interfacing

We have been using fusible interfacings since they were developed in 1968 by the Armo interfacing company, for which Pati Palmer and Susan Pletsch worked. Fusible interfacings have come a long way since then! Gone are the stiff, bake-on, fall-off interfacings of the past.

Today's fusibles are not bulky, so they can be included in seams. They stabilize, eliminating stretch in bias areas such as the roll line. Fusibles have a thermoplastic coating, so can be fused flat, then reheated to create the desired roll in the lapel and collar. Hems are interfaced with fusibles, so catch stitching a hair canvas in a hemline is not necessary. Fusibles help darts press better and they add body to hem areas.

Where to Interface

When in doubt, interface! Most garments look terrific when brand new, but interfaced garments still look great years later.

Edges get a lot more wear in a jacket than in a blouse, so the front is interfaced. This also gives pockets more support. Hems on pieces not underlined with fusible are interfaced as well.

Details such as pockets and collars need extra body. Interfacing also supports details like buttonholes.

21

Fusibles vs. Sew-ins

There are so many interfacings out there, we know there is a lot of confusion. We will direct you the best we can, but you can also ask experienced sewers in fabric stores for recommendations. And remember, fashion influences how firm or soft the interfacing should be.

SEW-IN INTERFACINGS

Some fabrics, such as napped fabrics like velvet or textured fabrics like seersucker, work better with a sew-in interfacing, as fusing can change the look of the fabric. Also, fusibles won't adhere to fabrics with a high triacetate fiber content. An easy way to interface these fabrics is to use a fusible on an underlining and glue the underlining to the fashion fabric. See page 26.

Woven sew-ins work in both woven and knit fabrics. Nonwoven sew-ins may "buckle" in enclosed areas such as collars in woven fabrics. They don't contract with the fabric, but can expand or stretch, making them compatible with knits. Stable nonwovens are used to stabilize welt pockets. For sleeve heads in jackets we use either a polyester woven tie interfacing or a nonwoven polyester fleece.

FUSIBLE INTERFACINGS

For most fabrics, fusible interfacings give the best look in the least amount of time. Today's fusibles can be used with nearly every fabric because of the new fusible resins.

Our favorite are weft-insertion interfacings, which are actually knits with a yarn woven in the weft (crosswise) direction. These have the drapability of a knit and the crosswise stability of a woven.

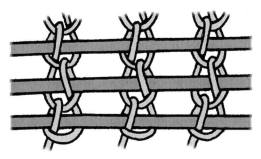

a weft-insertion under a microscope

How to Choose a Fusible Interfacing

MAKE A TEST SAMPLE

You will need to have a collection of interfacings to choose from to test with your fabrics. We always buy an assortment to have on hand. After you cut your garment, test several interfacings on a scrap of fabric. For a jacket with a sewn-on facing, we sew two interfaced scraps together, trim, and press to see how an edge will look. Also, you now have a sample on which to test a buttonhole.

jacket front—a heavier interfacing   *facing—two choices of lighter interfacings*

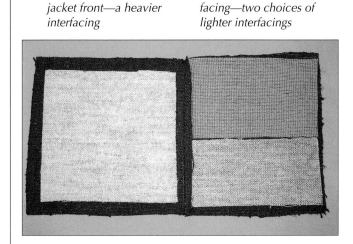

CHECK YOUR SAMPLE FOR:

◆ **Outside appearance**. Is there a color change or does the interfacing show through the fabric?

◆ **Feel**. Do the fabric and interfacing feel good together? Is it stiff? Or too soft? Use different weights on your test sample. Which combination feels the best?

◆ **Washability**. Toss the test sample in the washer and dryer if you plan to wash the garment.

◆ **Color**. Use white interfacing whenever possible. This makes it easier to see markings and the seam when we have to unstitch mistakes. Test to be sure it does not show through a dark fabric. If you are sewing machine buttonholes in a dark fabric, use dark interfacing in the fronts.

The PerfectFuse™ Solution

Several years ago Pati and Marta found some interfacing products to be inconsistent, others to be stiff, and some to bubble. So in 2000 they developed their own interfacing line. Their goal was to make it simple but work in most fabrics and for most interfacing needs.

Pati and Marta had several criteria:

◆ **Simplification** - There are so many interfacing choices that the customer has no idea what to use where. They narrowed the choices to four.

◆ **Easy-to-see differences** - Often, you can't tell the difference visually between one interfacing and another. Their four are different in appearance.

◆ **Good performance** - Some interfacings bubble during laundering or abrade and pill. Weft interfacings do not do this.

◆ **Wider widths** - These new interfacings are 60" and 66" wide, TWICE the width of most other interfacings, which must be pieced in some garments.

◆ **Good instructions** - Each of the new interfacings has its own instructions for both use and care. In addition, each package includes well-researched and well-written general instructions for using fusibles.

◆ **Less confusion in your interfacing stash at home** -These come in well-marked protective storage bags that keep the interfacing clean and identifiable. The bags contain one or three yard lengths.

◆ **Quality** - Consumers haven't had much confidence how interfacings will perform. Pati and Marta tested hundreds of products over a four-year period and spent two years writing, editing, and testing use and care instructions.

PerfectFuse Sheer: (60" wide) Perfect for slippery or smooth fabrics for a sheer, but crisp hand. Use in collars and cuffs on dresses, shirts and blouses. Sheer can be fused to cotton batiste or silk organza to give underlining more body. It is also nice on hard-to-fuse fabrics like some wool gabardines or microfibers. This all-polyester interfacing does not need to be preshrunk. (Sheerweft, 150 cm wide, in Australia.)

Sheer and Light are the same weight, but Light is a softer more open weave. Sheer is more crisp when fused.

SHEER	LIGHT

PerfectFuse Light: (60" wide) This is the interfacing used by the garment industry to add body to soft fabrics. Use with dress-weight silks, rayons or handwovens and in combination with PerfectFuse Tailor to add body to the sides and back on fabrics like wool crepe, linen and silk suiting. It can also be used on facings and the upper collar. It is all polyester and does not need to be preshrunk. (Textureweft, 150 cm wide, in Australia.)

PerfectFuse Medium: (60" wide) This midweight is often used on the facing and upper collar to add extra body, or on unconstructed or unlined jackets. It is also perfect for Ultrasuede fabrics. Medium is a rayon/polyester blend, and should be preshrunk. (Whisperweft, 120 cm wide, Australia.)

PerfectFuse Tailor: (66" wide) The interfacing for blazer jackets. Use to fuse the whole jacket front and under collar. The interfacing is 66" wide, and one yard is enough for two jackets in most sizes. This is also a rayon/polyester blend and should be preshrunk. (Armoweft, 120 cm wide, in Australia.)

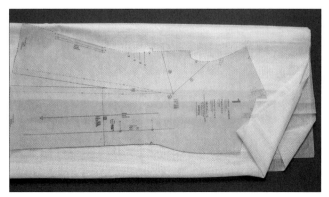

One yard of 66"-wide PerfectFuse Tailor makes four layers to fuse the entire front of two jackets.

General Recommended Choices

FOR LIGHTWEIGHT FABRICS

(cotton, silk, rayon, Tencel®, chambray) Fuse all pieces with PerfectFuse Light or Sheer, testing first. Fusing to the sleeves is optional. Also, stabilize handwoven fabrics with PerfectFuse Light or Sheer. Add a sew-in across the back.

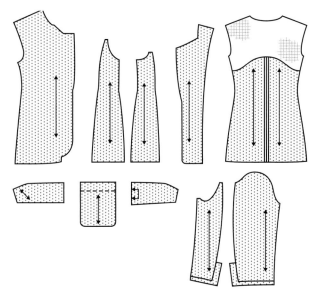

FOR MEDIUM-WEIGHT FABRICS

(wool crepe, wool gabardine, silk suiting, linen, denim) Fuse PerfectFuse Tailor to the front and under collar and PerfectFuse Light to the upper collar, facings, back, side panels, pockets, and bias strips in sleeve hems. Add a sew-in across the back.

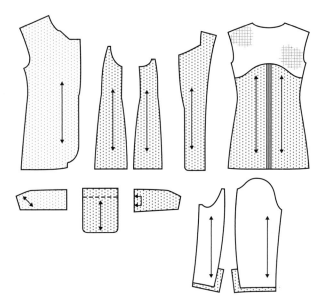

FOR HEAVY-WEIGHT FABRICS

(wool tweed, wool flannel, heavy silk tweed) Fuse front and under collar with PerfectFuse Tailor. Use bias PerfectFuse Medium in hems. Use a sew-in across the back. Exception: for coats and unconstructed jackets, we generally just interface the under collar and front facing.

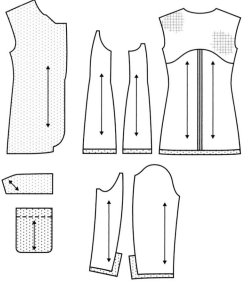

U.S. Product		Name in Australia
PerfectFuse Sheer		Sheerweft
PerfectFuse Light		Textureweft
PerfectFuse Medium		Whisperweft
PerfectFuse Tailor		Armoweft

See Chapter 3, Fabrics, for specific interfacing suggestions for different fabrics.

PRO Tip Always make a TEST SAMPLE!

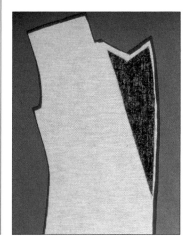

You can fuse on top of another fusible when you want extra body such as in a peaked lapel. Fuse up to the roll line and make the uppermost layer slightly smaller than the first layer so it won't be noticeable.

Add body to an under collar in the stand area (below the roll line) by fusing another layer, cut on the crosswise grain, on top of the seamed under collar. (See page 77.)

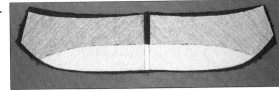

Sewn-In Interfacings

Some fabrics, such as velvet, seersucker, and many evening fabrics, work better with a sewn-in interfacing. We also prefer a sew-in for the back stay in jackets. Fusing the back stay may leave a visible line across the back.

These are possible sew-in interfacings:

◆ **Poly/cotton or muslin** - perfect for the back stay. Cut on a fold and baste to the back after the center back seam is sewn. (See page 76.)

◆ **Silk organza** - a wonderful underlining for dry cleanable fabrics needing more body or when you wish to fuse interfacing to the underlining. (It is also used as the "window" facing in Marta's favorite bound buttonhole. See page 109.)

◆ **Cotton batiste** - used the same way as silk organza, but washable. When used as an underlining, add PerfectFuse Sheer as an interfacing for extra body.

When using these for interfacing, test by making a sandwich of the layers and feeling to see if they are compatible. The interfacing should complement the fashion fabric, not overpower it.

 Glue-baste sew-in shaping fabrics to fashion fabric.

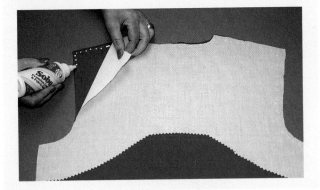

Lining

The finishing touch, the lining layer can be as gorgeous or functional as you want it to be. A lining should cover the inside construction, so an opaque fabric is important. A slick fabric makes putting on and taking off the garment easier. A lining fabric should be as long-wearing as the fashion fabric. (Relining a jacket or coat is NOT FUN!)

For functional purposes, we like polyester linings. They wear forever, are easy to handle, and maintain their shape. Use a polyester faille or crepe for a luxury look. Hang Loose and Hang Free (60"-wide with a rayon feel) by Logantex and Sun Silky in Australia are anti-static.

For summer comfort we often choose rayon, acetate, or rayon/acetate blends. Our favorite rayon is Ambiance by Logantex. These fabrics are not quite as durable or as washable, but they have the advantage of being made of fibers that breathe.

For fun, forget about trying to match the fashion fabric, and find a contrasting lining that will add flair! Blouse-weight prints are super and you can make a matching shirt or dress.

Print ties together two woolens

Silk print adds pizazz to beige wool

Look for a small print that blends well with anything. Stripes, dots, checks, and small two-color prints are very versatile. Even in conservative menswear, linings are often bold and gorgeous. We saw a black gabardine business suit with a smashing RED PLAID lining!

 Susan has a beautiful silk scarf that she plans to recycle into a jacket lining. The scarf is large enough to line the jacket body and she will find a coordinating solid fabric for the sleeves.

Underlining

Choose underlining fabric by the amount of body needed to create the look you want from your fashion fabric. As fashion changes from more shaped to softer silhouettes, you may still want to use an underlining. It will make light-colored fabric opaque and will give a layer to which you can invisibly hand stitch hems and shoulder pads. You can use a fusible or a sew-in underlining fabric such as silk organza or cotton batiste. Today, most ready-made clothing has a fused underlining.

Basting a sew-in underlining in place is tedious and there is the chance of the underlining slipping while sewing. What is the answer? Use a liquid fabric glue that dries fairly clearly and softly. It can be found in most sewing notions departments.

1. Place your fabric on a flat padded pressing surface. Steam press all the wrinkles out. Place your underlining on top and steam press the two together. This removes wrinkles and any further shrinkage.

2. Lift underlining and dot fabric glue on fashion fabric close to the edge **in the seam allowances**. Pat the two layers together. Allow 5 minutes to dry.

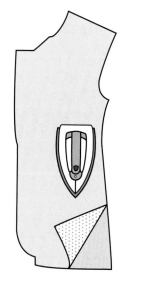 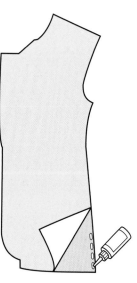

NOTE: For more underlining information, including the "Glue and Fold" technique, see *Mother Pletsch's Painless Sewing*, by Pati Palmer and Susan Pletsch.

Interlining (Optional)

An interlining is the layer sewn to the wrong side of the lining to add extra warmth to a coat or jacket. It should add warmth but not weight, so look for a lightweight but lofty fabric. Following are some suggestions:

- A loosely woven wool - dry clean only
- Pellon Polyester Fleece or Thermolam - washable nonwoven fleece
- Outing flannel - a washable cotton or cotton/polyester flannel (be sure to preshrink!)
- Armo-Rite - lofty woven washable polyester/rayon tie interfacing (similar to lamb's wool, which is no longer available)
- Polyester needlepunch

Some lining fabrics are self-interlined:
- Pre-quilted fabrics
- Millium® - an insulated lining
- Fleece-backed lining

The easiest way to interline is to stitch the interlining to the lining—in other words, to underline the lining! Since the interlining occupies some of the inside ease, it is usually placed in the body of the garment but not in the sleeves.

1. Cut interlining from lining pattern pieces, omitting back pleat and hem.
2. Temporarily baste center back pleat in lining closed. Pin corresponding lining/interlining pieces together and machine baste all edges 1/2" from the edge.
3. Assemble lining as pattern suggests.
4. Trim bulky interlining close to stitching line.
5. Stitch lining into garment as directed in Chapter 13, or finish edges to zip or button in.

Preshrinking and Care of Shaping Fabrics

INTERFACINGS

You will need to test interfacings to select the one you like best. If your garment is washable, you should preshrink both your fabric and interfacing for realistic results in the test sample. Today's interfacings have only a 1-2% shrinkage factor, but your fashion fabric may have more or less.

Woven, weft, and knit fusibles, especially those containing rayon - Place in a basin of HOT water and soak for 10 minutes. It will not hurt the fusing agent, which is activated at 300 degrees or more. But do not agitate or you might dislodge some of the fusing resin. Roll in a towel and then hang over a towel rack to dry. Do not wad up or wring. Do not machine dry!

100% polyester weft fusibles do not need preshrinking. However, if you want to **wash** the finished garment, make a TEST sample to make sure you like the result. Minor puckers will generally press out. Wash finished garments gently by hand or in a gentle cycle in the washer. Clothing looks new longer if hanger dried.

If you plan to **dry-clean** the finished garment, pre-steam the interfacing. Place the interfacing resin side down on the wrong side of the fashion fabric. Hold your iron 2" above the interfacing and steam for three or four seconds in each area. You may see some interfacings shrink as you steam. A "shot-of-steam" type iron works best.

Non-woven fusibles - There is no need to preshrink in water. If these shrink at all, it is the steam from your iron that causes it. Try "steam shrinking" as described above.

Woven sew-ins - Most only have a 1-2% shrinkage factor. However, it is best to preshrink to ensure compatibility with your preshrunk fashion fabric. Preshrink using the same method you plan to clean the finished garment. If washing, use detergent. If dry-cleaning your finished garment, generally heavily steaming the interfacing is adequate.

LININGS

Preshrink washable linings in the washer and dryer. Preshrink hand-washable linings by the dunk method above. You do not need to preshrink linings in garments you plan to dry-clean. Dryer sheets can leave spots on polyester linings.

Common Questions About Fusibles

Does fusible interfacing give the same result as hand stitches in custom tailoring?

Yes! Today's fusibles are used by the best European and American designers and have the same look as we had 30 years ago with all the hand work, but are so much faster!

Why do I get bubbles with fusing?

Bubbles can occur for two reasons. A bubble in your fashion fabric generally means the interfacing shrank more than the fashion fabric. You will have shrinkage with wool, even if it was preshrunk, because so much steam is needed to fuse. Bubbles in the interfacing generally indicate places where the iron was not applied long enough to fuse properly. Even fusing requires careful overlapping, with the iron set on wool and steam.

Why would I want to use more than one type of interfacing in the same jacket?

Combinations of interfacing provide versatility. You may want a heavier interfacing in the front and a lighter or softer weight fusible in the hems, facings and pockets. We suggest using a sew-in for the back interfacing or stay. Sometimes it is necessary to layer interfacings for extra body.

What causes those ugly "polka dots" in fused areas on the right side of the fabric that appear after laundering?

"Strike-through" is caused by using the wrong fusible on the fabric. It happens more with smooth or lightweight fabrics, not with heavier fabrics. Choosing a different interfacing will solve the problem.

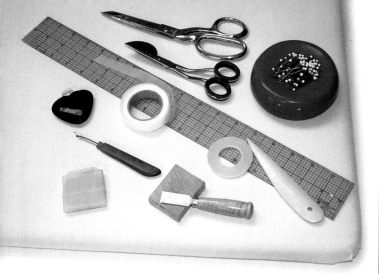

Have these sewing aids on hand at all times—especially for tailoring!

CUTTING AND MARKING TOOLS

- **Pins** - Use 1 3/8″ long, extra-fine glass-head pins and store in a magnetic pin holder.
- **Sewing gauge** (6″ ruler) - marks hems and buttonholes
- **8-9″ bent-handled shears** (in good sharp condition) - The blades glide along the table as you cut.
- **Pinking shears** - seam finish for unlined jacket
- **Duck-bill scissors**, embroidery scissors, or tailor points - for ripping/clipping/snipping/trimming
- **Water-soluble or air-erasable marking pens** - Be sure to read the directions to avoid permanent staining.
- **Cutting board** - Make a "cut 'n press" board from particle board and natural fiber pad covered with muslin. Directions for making one can be found in these books:

- **See-through ruler** - helps place pattern onto fabric (Marta loves the 1″ x 12″ Olfa ruler.)
- **Basting tape** - 1/8″-wide (3mm) double-faced tape used in place of pins or hand basting
- **A full-length and a hand-held mirror (for the rear view)** - Save fitting time by having them in your sewing room.

- **Seam ripper** - the best friend you can have
- **Stay-tape®** - a lightweight stabilized tricot used to prevent bias edges from stretching or to stabilize the roll line
- **Tailor's chalk wheel or chalk with holder**—The chalk wheel is easier for marking, but disappears quickly, so immediately stitch on the line. Use hard chalk when you need the markings to last longer.
- **Gridded cardboard** - The grid makes layout easier. They come folded or as tables.
  USA - The Sew/Fit table is available with legs in two heights, 34″ and 40″. We have had 30 of them in our classroom for 12 years and none have had to be replaced. They are made by:
  Quilter's Rule
  817 Mohr Ave., Waterford, WI 53185
  262/514-2000. Fax 262/514-2100.
  AUSTRALIA - There is a similar product from:
  Baraque School of Sewing,
  77G Roland Ave, Wahroonga, NSW 2076
  02 9487 1177

SEWING TOOLS

- **Buttonhole cutter** - a sharp blade on a stick with a wooden block for precise cutting of machine buttonholes
- **Fabric glue** - liquid glue for glue-basting underlining
- **Universal needles** - (size 80/12 for most fabrics) They prevent skipped stitches.
- **Fusible web** 1/4″-wide (6mm) roll or Steam-A-Seam® (1/4″ wide) - for placing patch pockets
- **Point turner** - Turns corners right side out.

CHAPTER 6
Pressing

Pressing is second only to fitting in importance for the quality look of a finished garment. A myriad of problems can be rectified with steam and heat. "Press as you sew" has been preached for years, but nowhere is it quite as important as in tailoring. Please don't think you can ignore pressing and pay your cleaners to press after you've finished. Cleaners can often do a nice final press—but how can they possibly get inside your jacket after it's completed? So move the ironing board next to your sewing machine; adjust the board to machine table height; and then sew, swivel, press; sew, swivel, press.

Pressing Equipment

Don't even consider making a tailored garment unless you have (or are willing to purchase) some basic pressing equipment.

THE ABSOLUTE ESSENTIALS

Steam iron - Look for one with lots of holes. We like the "shot-of-steam" types with a button to push for a jet of steam that will press even the most stubborn fabric. A steam generator iron is a luxury, and if you sew a lot, it will spoil you. It holds lots of water in a separate tank and will steam even when the the sole plate is set at a lower temperature because the steam is generated in the tank, not the iron. It steams horizontally or vertically.

Pressing ham (tailor's ham) - a ham-shaped surface ideal for pressing curved and shaped areas to give "people shape" to flat fabric. Match the curve of the garment to that of the ham.

Point presser/clapper - a wooden combination tool. The point is used to press seams and corners open. The bottom is used to flatten a seam by holding heat and steam in a fabric under pressure until it cools. Often used with a seam roll or ham. It is sometimes called a pounding block.

Seam roll - a sausage shaped gadget used to press open flat seams and cylinders like sleeves. The seam allowances fall over the edge of the roll and allow your iron to touch only the stitching line itself.

OPTIONAL AIDS

There are some fantastic pressing aids that we love for tailoring and hope you will try.

June Tailor Board - the most versatile pressing tool. This marvelous aid has several "can't live without" surfaces. The long curved edge is perfect for pressing open a curved collar seam or blazer front seam. The small curve just fits rounded collars or rounded lower front seams. The point presser end is the best way to press into collar points. The optional padded cover makes a useful raised pressing surface.

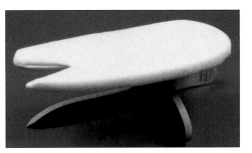

Press mitt - Have you ever wanted to press something on a hanger but didn't know how? Slip your hand into the press mitt and use your protected and shaped "hand" as your ironing board in the air.

See-through press cloth - a sheer cotton organdy press cloth that allows you to see what you're pressing and still protect the fabric.

 Fingers are FREE pressing tools! You can slightly finger press a seam or dart in the right direction BEFORE permanently pressing with the iron or use the wooden clapper to flatten.

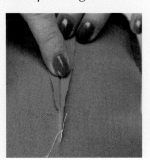

To find pressing supplies in Australia, check local fabric stores or for mail order try www.judisstudio.com.au.

How to Press

Pressing takes PATIENCE! Too-speedy pressing can create an overpressed, shiny, "I'm old and worn" look in a new garment. Synthetic fabrics will overpress more quickly than natural fabrics because the fibers are more heat-sensitive, so use a very light touch with these.

Also, **press, don't iron**. Pressing is lifting the iron when you move it. Ironing is sliding the iron on the fabric when you move it which can cause stretching.

 TEST YOUR FABRIC! To quickly see if a fabric will shine, form a pleat in a scrap and top-press. If the edge of the under layer makes a shiny line, you will need to use a press cloth to top-press!

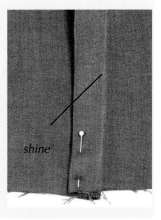
shine

Pressing Darts

1. Press darts flat first to flatten fold line and to eliminate any puckered stitching. If the fabric is bulky, clip the dart to within 1/2" (1.3cm) of the point and press open.

2. Press darts over a curve on a pressing ham that matches the curve of the dart and your body.

 The ham has many curves on it—one for every part of your body. Bust darts go over the very round curve at edge of ham, back shoulder darts over a flatter curve on top surface of ham.

If you don't press the dart open, tuck paper under the fold if necessary to prevent an indentation from showing on the right side.

3. Use a wooden clapper or your fingers to hold the dart down firmly, especially the point area, until the fabric cools.

Pressing Seams

Never cross a seam with another without pressing it first. Most pressing should be done from the inside to prevent possible shine. Top-press when construction pressing hasn't quite done the trick.

1. Press seams flat first over the stitches to remove any puckers.

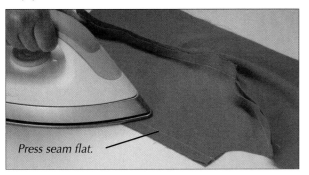

Press seam flat.

2. Press seams open over a seam roll or Seam Stick® (a long dowel cut in half lengthwise) to prevent seam imprints from showing on the right side. Press curved areas over matching curves on the ham. Saturate with steam.

Press a straight seam open over a seam roll.   *Press a curved seam open over a ham.*

3. Finger press or gently flatten the steamed seam with a wooden clapper. The wood cools the seam under pressure making it retain a crisp press. Let the fabric cool before moving.

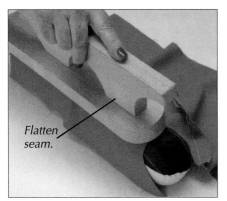

Flatten seam.

Pressing Edges

Here is the easy way to professional edges on collars, faced fronts, lapels, and collarless necklines!

1. Press seam as it was stitched.

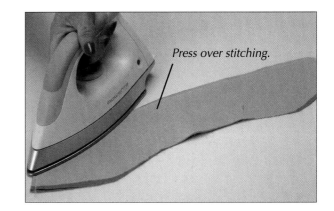

Press over stitching.

2. Carefully press seam open over seam roll, ham, top of point presser, or Tailor Board, whichever is the best fit.

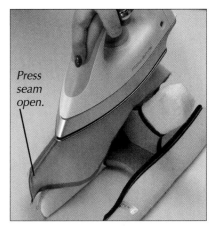

Press seam open.

3. Turn right side out and final press. Press from the under side which allows you to make sure the seam rolls to the under side.

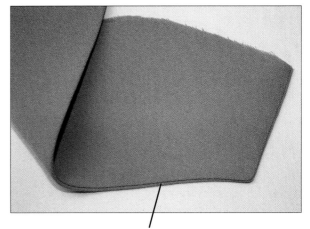

Be sure to roll the seam to the under side as you press.

CHAPTER 7

Make Sure It Will Fit

Pattern Size

Fitting is easier if you start with the right size pattern. Yet many women buy the wrong size. Patterns are made for the average B bra cup. If you are a DD and buy according to your full bust measurement, your pattern will be too large in the neck and shoulder area.

You need to take only ONE measurement to find your best size. It is called the "high bust" measurement. It eliminates the bust cup size factor.

It will get you the right fit in the shoulder area. If you are full busted, you will need to do the bust adjustment for your cup size. If your waist and hips are larger or smaller than the size you bought, you can easily adjust them to fit. Tissue-fitting will quickly tell you what to do! See our book *Fit For Real People* for complete fitting information.

STANDARD EASE TODAY

This changes a little with fashion. The following is the current bust ease allowed:

Fitted jacket (worn without a blouse or with a simple lightweight shell) - 2-3" ease (5-7.5cm)

Semi-fitted jacket—3-5" ease (7.5-12.5cm)

Classic blazer—5-7" ease (12.5-18cm)

Oversized jacket—8-18" ease (20.5-46cm)

A bust east of 5-7" may seem like a lot for a blazer. However, ease will be taken up by the layers of fabrics in the jacket and other clothing you wear under it. Ease is personal. You need to adjust a pattern for your own preferences. If you never plan to button a jacket, you may want less ease than if you wore it buttoned.

Also, keep in mind that when you buy a small (8-10), medium (12-14), large (16-18), or extra large (20-22), the pattern is cut for the larger of the two sizes. These patterns also generally have more ease.

3½" (9cm) bust
6½" (16.3cm) hip ease

4½" (11.5cm) bust
5½" (14cm) hip ease

Ease

Pattern companies automatically build in the extra ease needed for a coat or jacket to be worn over other clothes. See how the garment is shown on the pattern envelope. If a coat is shown worn over a jacket, then enough extra ease has been allowed for that purpose.

Determine the amount of ease you like in a jacket. Try on a jacket you currently have in your wardrobe.

"Quick Pinch Test":
Pinch the body and sleeve of a jacket to check the ease in a garment. If you pinch 2" (5cm) that means that your jacket has 4" (10cm) of ease at that spot. (You are pinching a double thickness of fabric.) Be sure you are pinching only one side and pulling all the fabric to that side.

Most jackets have between 3-6" bust ease. But perhaps a size 8 woman would be comfortable with 3" ease while a size 20 would prefer 5" ease. These amounts are only suggestions. Personal preferences may be more or less ease.

We love patterns that have finished garment measurements on the back of the envelope. Subtract the finished measurement from the body measurement to determine the ease in that design. Below are different styles with the amount of bust and hip ease in each.

5½" (14cm) bust
6½" (16.3cm) hip ease

8½" (21.8cm) bust
9½" (24.3cm) hip ease

Photos courtesy of McCall Pattern Company

33

How to Fit a Pattern

Try on the Pattern

Trim outside the black cutting line to remove excess tissue. Press pattern with a warm dry iron. Mark the 5/8" seamlines so you can accurately pin the pattern pieces together.

Tape the curved areas so the pattern won't tear when you try it on. Use small pieces of tape around the curves, lapping the short pieces. Use 1/2" (1.3mm) Scotch™ Magic™ Tape (green box). Clip the curves to the tape in neck and armhole area. DO NOT CUT THROUGH TAPE.

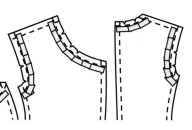

Gently tug on the tissue to make sure it won't tear.

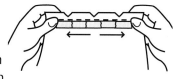

Pin in darts and pin the seams together with seam allowances pinned to the outside.

Try the pattern on over the same type of clothes you'll wear under the finished garment.

Pull the tissue snugly over your bust, but if the pattern won't reach your center front or center back, check and alter the back first, and then do a bust alteration.

When all the alterations are complete, you should be able to pin the pattern center front and back to your center front and back —to your clothes that is! Slip in a shoulder pad.

FIT Tip

We prefer raglan shoulder pads even in set-in sleeves, because they act like your shoulder. You can move the pad in or out to widen or narrow your shoulders to create a flattering body proportion. See page 89 for more.

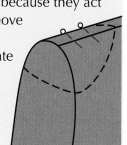

Tissue-Fitting and Common Alterations

Waist Length

If the waist marking on the pattern is above or below your waist, lengthen or shorten all pieces above the waist.

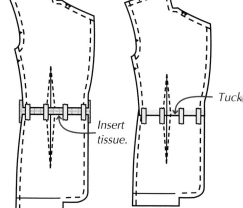

Insert tissue.

Tuck

Broad or Narrow Back

Check the back width first. Why? If you have a broad back, the tissue won't come to your center front. Fix the back before checking the front. Be sure the armhole seam is at the crease in your arm (where sleeve seam will be) before measuring at the center back.

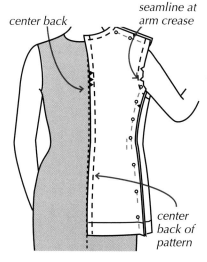

center back

seamline at arm crease

center back of pattern

Broad Back

Cut the back through the shoulder to the hemline. After spreading back, true the stitching and cutting lines at the shoulder. Do not add at the center back or the neck will be too large.

You will need to ease the back shoulder to fit the front or add a shoulder dart.

Perfect Pattern Paper is gridded and the same weight as the tissue —a perfect altering companion!

Narrow Back

To make the back narrower, make a full length tuck through the back shoulder seam to the hem. Then, widen back shoulder until it matches the front.

High Round Back

This is a very common alteration today, even for young people, due to hunching over a computer. If the neck seam does not come to the base of your neck (where a necklace would sit), cut about 1″ (2.5cm) below the neck seam to the shoulder or armhole edge and raise the upper back 1/4″ to 3/8″ (6mm to 1cm). Fill in space with tissue.

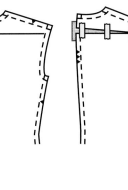

Very Round Back

(Ask a friend to help.)

1. Draw a horizontal line on the tissue 6-8″ (15-20.5cm) from the neck.

2. Pin front to back. Try on.

3. Pull the tissue down at the center back until the line is straight. Tape the tissue to your skin below the line.

4. Slash tissue from center back to the armhole seam. Raise upper back tissue to your neck. Tape across the opening to keep the adjustment.

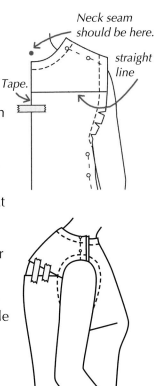

Neck seam should be here.

Tape.

straight line

5. Remove the pattern. Unpin. Place on top of alteration tissue. Make sure pattern lies flat. Re-tape if necessary.

6. If the pattern was to be cut on the fold, add a seam allowance to the center back and sew the seam to the curve of your body.

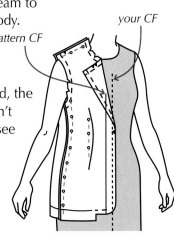

Trim away excess tissue.

Full Bust

If you are full-busted, the pattern center front won't match yours. You may see a gap in the armhole. **Extend the pattern's center front line up to your bust level** so measuring is easier.

Try on the tissue. Make sure the center back is at yours. Raise your arm and pull tissue firmly toward your center front. Lower your arm to anchor tissue. Measure straight across from the pattern center front to yours.

your CF

pattern CF

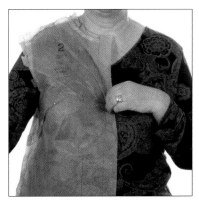

For less fitted jackets, don't push in to your skin or force the tissue to the CF. You will see drag lines from the shoulder.

For the amount to alter the pattern, measure from the pattern's center front to yours. The pattern should be pulled firmly, but not tightly, across your front so that you don't over-alter for a full bust, especially if you plan to wear your jacket unbuttoned.

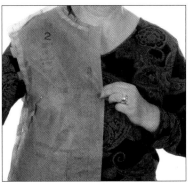

When it hangs straight from the shoulder, the pattern CF doesn't come to Marta's CF. A bust alteration is needed after all for a better fit.

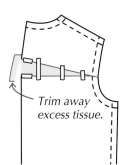

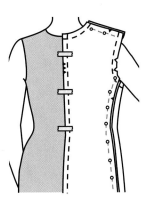

1. Find pattern's apex (bust point). The pattern usually has an arrow or a ⊕ at the pattern's apex.

2. Draw line 1 on your pattern from the hem edge to the apex, parallel to the grainline, then to the armhole notch.

3. Draw line 2 about 2-3" below the armhole to the apex or through the center of the horizontal dart.

4. Draw line 3 above the lower front curve.

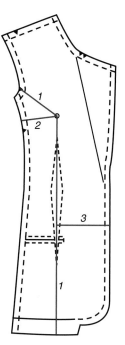

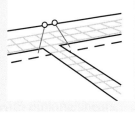

Angle pins AWAY from the center of the cut tissue section so the tissue can't move.

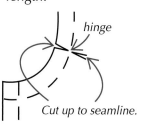

5. Cut on line 1 from the lower edge up to, but not through, the armhole seam. Cut on line 2 from the side to, but not through, the apex.

Don't cut to the edge of the pattern or the seamline will change in length.

hinge

Cut up to seamline.

Cut to the seamline from both sides forming a "hinge" at the seamline. The seamline is then the same length after spreading.

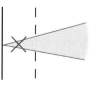

spread

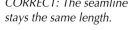
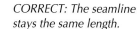

INCORRECT: The seamline spreads.

CORRECT: The seamline stays the same length.

Pattern tissue overlaps in seam allowance.

Pin the areas to the right of line 1 to a cardboard cutting board to hold it in place.

6. Pull the side section apart along line 1 the amount you determined during fitting, keeping the long edges of line 1 parallel. To do this and keep the pattern TOTALLY FLAT, **the armhole goes up and the side panel drops down** (vertical arrows). Line 2 opens up, forming a **new** or deeper dart. Now anchor the sections with pins as shown.

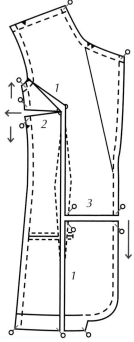

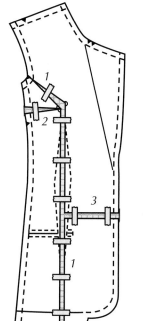

7. Cut on line 3. Spread until the bottom edges of the pattern sections are even. Anchor as shown.

8. Fill line 1, 2, and 3 with tissue. Redraw pocket and dart lines.

Redraw Vertical Darts

When line 1 goes through a vertical bust dart. Keep the stitching line closest to the center front and draw a new stitching line on the other side the same distance from line 1. Disregard the original stitching line closer to the side seam.

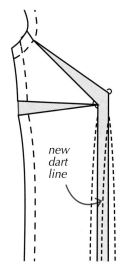

new dart line

Raise or Lower Darts

After altering your tissue, pin in the darts and pin front to back. Try on. Mark your bust point (X).

Raise or lower the dart point until it points to the "X". Redraw to new point.

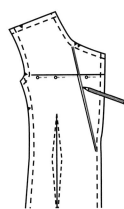

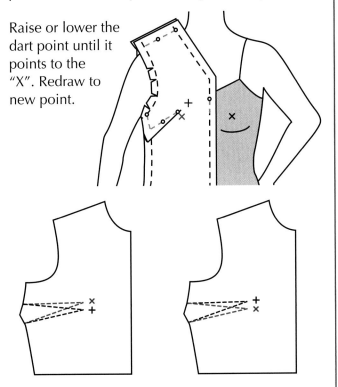

OR, you can draw a box around the dart and cut it out. Raise or lower until dart points to the "X".

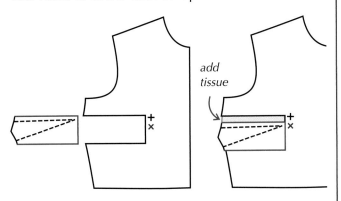

add tissue

The dart point should stop 1/2" (small bust) to 1½" (large bust) from the bust point. You may need to shorten or lengthen the point of the dart.

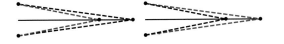

See page 47 for altering for princess full bust.

Front Gap

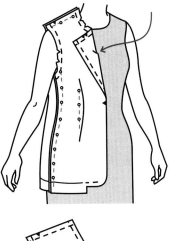

If the lapel gaps, make a tuck in front and front facing from outer edge of lapel to nothing at the armhole. Draw two lines and tape them together. True the roll line. See Sue Neall on page 49.

Full Hips

If you need more hip room, tape tissue to the side seams of the pattern and pin to fit your body. If the pattern has a side panel, add tissue to both sides of the side panel as well as to the sides of the front and back. When you try on the pattern, pin seams to fit you. You might need to add more to the side front seam than the side back seam. It will depend on your shape.

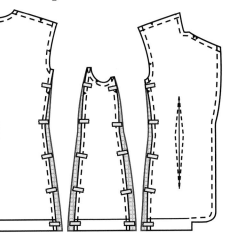

 Use Perfect Pattern Paper. Make sure to place the grid on both front and back pieces exactly the same so it is easy to add the same amount to both pieces when pin-fitting to your body shape.

Sway/Flat Back

If your side seam swings forward and the pattern hangs longer at the center back, take a tuck just above the waist tapering to nothing at the side seam until back is level and side seam is straight.

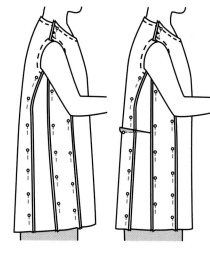

If the back is in two pieces, lap the seamlines and draw a "V". Fold the lines together in each piece separately and tape.

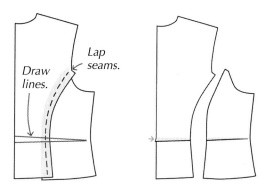

Draw lines. *Lap seams.*

The average amount removed is about 1/2" (1.3cm), but if it is 3/4" (2cm) or more, make two separate smaller tucks, one above the other.

The horizontal tuck will distort the grainline on the pattern. To straighten, connect the arrow points with a new vertical line.

If the garment has a center back seam, it will be slightly curved which is fine. Or, straighten the cut edge if you'd prefer.

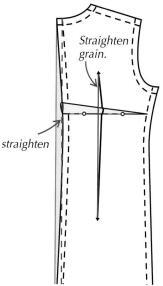

Straighten grain.

straighten

If the center back is cut on the fold, the waist area won't touch the fold, but the added width is minor and won't negatively affect the overall fit.

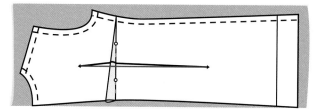

Square or Sloping Shoulders

Take shallower or deeper seam at outer edge of shoulder to the normal seamline at the neckline. Raise or lower the underarm the same amount.

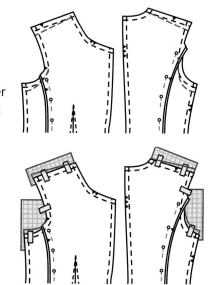

 FIT Tip Another way to adjust is to use thicker or thinner shoulder pads than the pattern calls for.

Forward Shoulder

The use of computers and sitting at desks has contributed to a new fit phenomenon for all ages, the forward shoulder. If your clothes won't stay on your shoulders, you are a candidate.

Look at your shoulder seam. Is it in the center of your arm?

Alter the pattern by pivoting the shoulder seam forward. Trim the excess tissue from the front and add to the back to make new 5/8" (1.5cm) seam allowances.

seam should be here

The dot on the sleeve cap will be matched to the new shoulder position. It may be necessary to ease a bit more of the front of the sleeve cap into the front armhole. (We haven't needed to rotate sleeves since we began correcting the shoulder!)

FRONT   *BACK*

Broad or Narrow Shoulders

Take the back and front shoulders in or let them out as shown.

Sleeve Width and Length

Pin the sleeve to the jacket at the underarm ONLY. Try on. Pinch the tissue where your upper arm is fullest. If you can't pinch an inch, the sleeve is too tight.

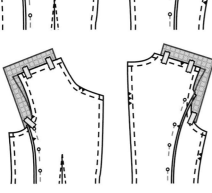

Common Sleeve Alterations

What follows are common sleeve alterations. For the more unusual ones, see our book *Fit for Real People*.

FULL ARMS

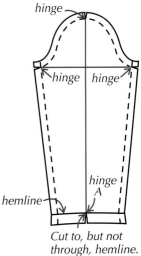

hinge
hinge *hinge*
hemline
hinge
A
Cut to, but not through, hemline.

1. Draw a straight line from the shoulder dot to the hemline. Draw a perpendicular line connecting the underarm seams.

2. Cut on these lines to, but not through, seams and hemline. See "hinge" page 36. Anchor at A with pins in hemline.

3. Spread the amount needed at arrow by pulling underarms apart. Do not tape yet!

4. Anchor with pins at B, and then at C.

5. Make sure the tissue is totally flat, then anchor the top of the cap and where the tissue laps.

6. Insert tissue under the open area and tape in place.

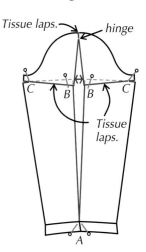

Tissue laps.   *hinge*
C *B* *B* *C*
Tissue laps.
A

THIN ARMS

If your arms are thin, jacket sleeves may feel too large, especially if the style is oversized.

Slash as for full arms, but lap the pieces at the center rather than spreading them.

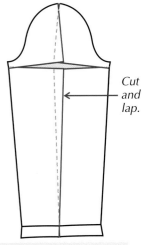

Cut and lap.

 Quick Tip To find the underarm line on the upper sleeve of a 2-piece sleeve, lap the pieces as shown. Alter the UPPER sleeve only.

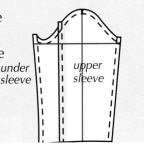

under sleeve   *upper sleeve*

CAP HEIGHT

If you need to spread a sleeve more than 1" (2.5cm), you may need to raise the cap back to its original height.

1. Trace the original cap from notch to notch onto tissue before altering.

2. Make the alteration. Use the original sleeve cap cutting line, allowing some "in-case" seam allowance for fitting. You will probably need only about half of the extra height.

SLEEVE LENGTH

Check sleeve length. If the sleeve is not the right length, cut and spread to lengthen or tuck to shorten on all pieces. This can be done above and below the elbow if necessary for a shaped sleeve. See page 80 for sleeve length.

Fitting as You Sew

After you have cut out the jacket, pin the side and shoulder seams **wrong sides together** placing pins along the stitching line. Pin darts on the outside so you can easily change them if necessary. Try on right side out since right and left sides of the body may be different.

Also, it may be necessary to take in or let out one side seam more than the other.

PRO Tip If the fabric is stretchy or loosely woven, the neckline should be staystitched so that it won't stretch (page 77). You should not hang the jacket on a hanger until the collar is stitched on.

Adjust the ease around the body by pinning deeper or shallower side seams.

You may also want to take in each side seam 1/8" - 1/4" at the waist to slenderize and create a slightly more hourglass illusion.

Also, it may be necessary to take in or let out one seam more than another.

Let out RIGHT side back seam here.

NOTE: After you have made all your adjustments, mark new seam lines. Spread open seam allowances and mark at pins on wrong side of garment using tailors' chalk, or water-soluble marking pen or marking pencil.

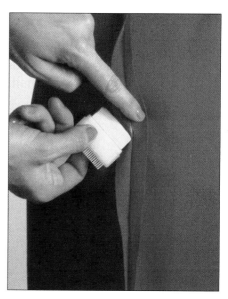

NOTE: See the Palmer/Pletsch *Fit for Real People* book for in-depth fitting help.

CHAPTER 8

Fitting Jackets on REAL People

Marta

Co-author Marta Alto has most of the common fitting problems. She will show how she alters a darted jacket and one with princess seams.

Classic Blazer

The Front Before

Marta has extended the center front line on the tissue into the lapel to make measuring easier. Marta pulls the pattern firmly across her bust. The pattern center front doesn't reach hers in either the bust or hip area. Before we can decide the size of the full bust alteration, we need to check her back. If she has a broad back, doing that alteration will bring the front closer to her center front.

The Back Before

The center back seamline is not coming to Marta's center back where we have placed a pin. This means she needs a broad back alteration.

The wrinkles also indicate she is rounded in the back. If we pull down on the pattern until the wrinkles disappear and the lines are horizontal, the distance from the pattern neck to hers would be the amount of additional length needed.

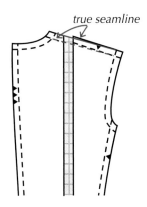

true seamline

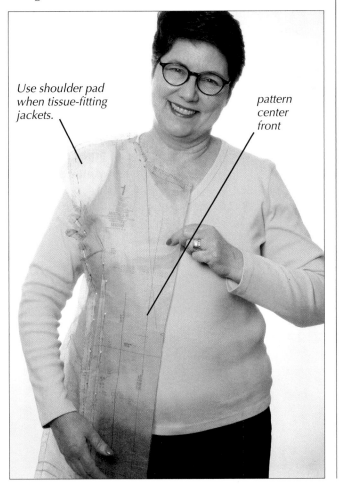

Use shoulder pad when tissue-fitting jackets.

pattern center front

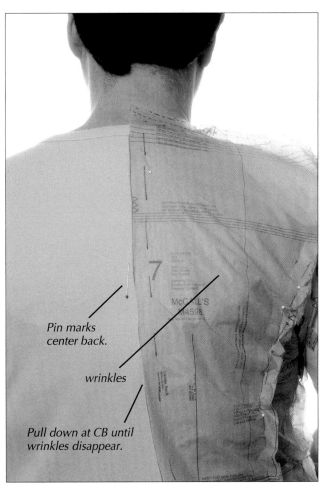

Pin marks center back.

wrinkles

Pull down at CB until wrinkles disappear.

The Back After

Marta has added to the back width until the center back seam line comes to her center back. Below the shoulder blades, the back swings toward the side. We will address that later. Adding to the hip width or taking a sway back tuck are solutions.

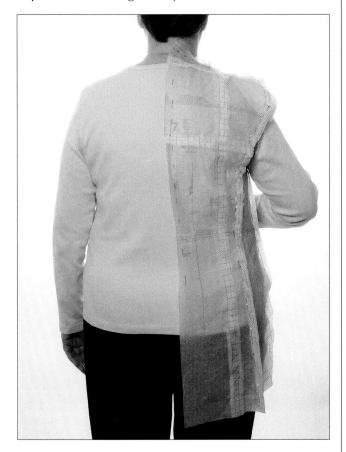

If you need more than 5/8" in back length, put that amount about 1" below the neckline seam and the rest in the shoulder blade area as shown. (See page 35.) Now it looks like the pattern is too long at the center back. This is because she is rounded in the upper back, but flat in the derriere. She fixed the upper back. We will deal with the lower back later.

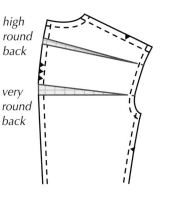

high round back

very round back

The Front After Back Alteration

The bust alteration: Draw lines as shown. Line 2 is where a bust dart would normally be, slanting up toward apex. Cut on line 1 up to armhole seam and line 2 up to but not through to line 1. Spread the front until you get the width you need. Line 2 will open up forming a dart. Cut on line 3 and make lower edges match.

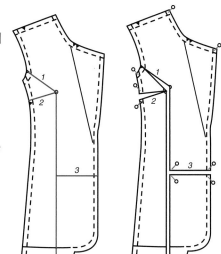

NOTE: This is not a princess style. The front has a side panel and is altered like any darted front. The horizontal bust dart was added when she widened the front the amount she needed for her full bust.

The Front After Bust Alteration

The pattern center front now comes to Marta's. AND the dart is in the right place and doesn't need to be raised or lowered. The wrinkles pointing to the vertical dart tell her to pin that dart narrower to allow for her tummy.

The Back After Sway Back Tuck

Marta now pins a tuck at the center back, making it hang straight.

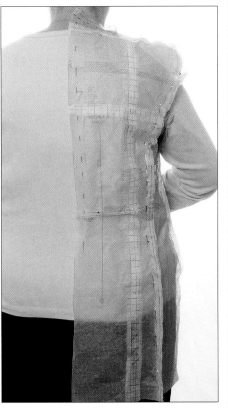

Since this is a 2-piece back, lap the back pattern pieces.

Draw a "V" the width you are removing at the center back, tapering to nothing at the side.

Then tuck each piece separately.

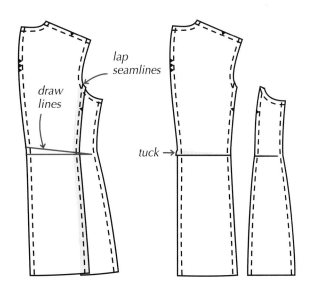

The Sleeve Shortened

The sleeve hem is turned up and the upper arm was shortened until the elbow ease area was at Marta's elbow.

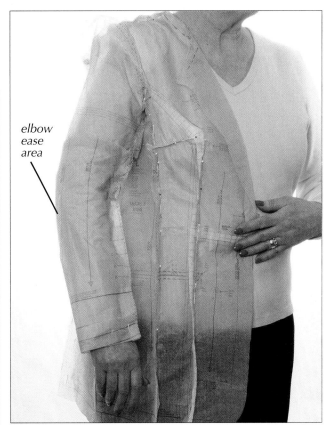

FABRIC FITTING

The Front Pinned in Fabric

Marta has pinned the seams on the outside so the fit is easier to "tweak." She is wearing a silky blouse she plans to wear with the finished jacket. She has slipped in shoulder pads. She feels the hips are too full so pinches in the side seams. The jacket looks great otherwise!

The Sleeve

Marta checks the sleeve for width and length. She has pinned the seams together and turned up the hem. She pins ONLY the underarm of the sleeve to the underarm of the jacket. If you pin the cap instead, you won't get the accurate length because the cap has extra height for ease or gathers.

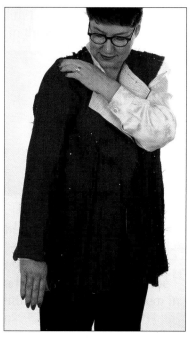

The Back Pinned in Fabric

The jacket back looks good. But since her right hip is fuller than her left, the center back seam is pulling to the right.

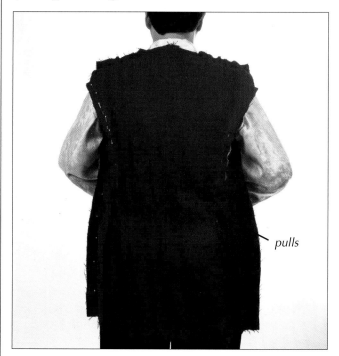

pulls

The Back Pinned in Fabric After

We let out the side back seam over her full high hip area and took a deeper seam in the left back hip area. Now the pulls are gone and the center back seam is straight.

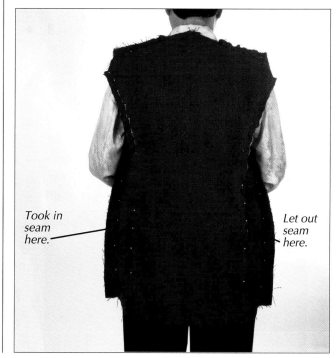

Took in seam here.

Let out seam here.

The Front Sewn

The pockets, shoulder and side seams, and under collar are sewn. The front looks PERFECT!

The Back Sewn After

Another layer of padding is added to the right shoulder. VOILA! The wrinkle is gone.

The right back hip was let out and the back is now totally smooth!

The Back Sewn Before

Marta is more sloping in her right shoulder which is causing a drag line in the fabric. There is also a little stress where her right back hip is fuller.

Drag line means it needs a deeper shoulder seam or extra layers of shoulder padding.

Wrinkles point to the problem. Marta needs to let seam out here for a little more room.

THE FINISHED BLAZER

Marta models her new jacket.

Princess-Style Cardigan

The Front Before

The jacket center front does not come to Marta's center front in either the bust or hip area. Before deciding if we need a bust and hip adjustment, we need to look at the back. If she has a broad back, doing that alteration will bring the front closer to her center front.

The Back Before

The center back seamline is not coming to Marta's center back where we have placed a pin. This means she needs a broad back alteration.

Pin is at center back.

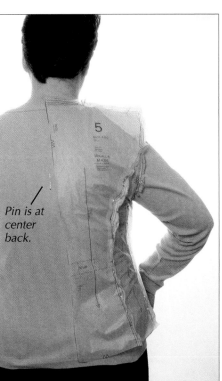

The Back After

Marta has added to the back width until the center back seam line comes to her center back. She also let out the side and side back seams in the hip area so the lower back would hang straight. She made high round back and round back alterations on the tissue as well.

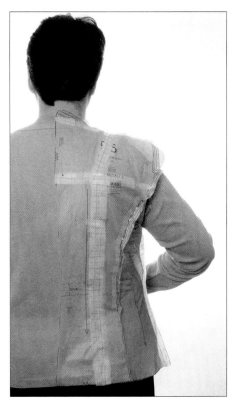

Measure for Bust Adjustment

Unpin the princess seam and match center fronts, then measure seam line to seam line at the bust to see how much to add. Marta needs 3/4" (2cm). For more on deciding whether to add to the side panel only or some to the front panel as well, see *Fit for Real People.*

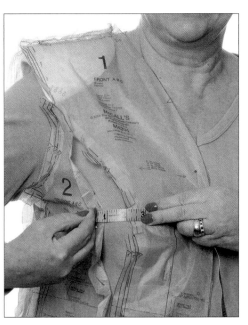

The Front After

To keep the princess seam centered over the bustline, Marta added width to both the side panel and front.

Marta's altered pattern fits well. Now she looks at the jacket length and feels it is too short for her. She will lengthen the pattern 2″ below the waist.

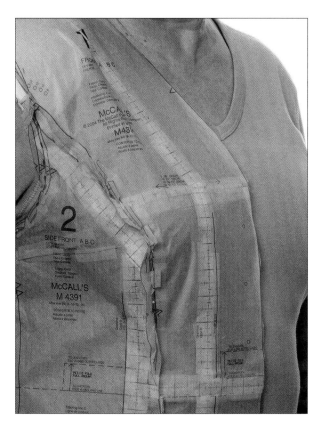

Marta widened the front first as shown. (The horizontal cut is to keep the bottom edge of the front pieces parallel.)

Then she made the same alterations described on page 36 to the side front.

Then she closed the dart and transferred it to line 4. She lengthened the front at line 5 equal to the opening at line 4, and line 6 equal to line 3.

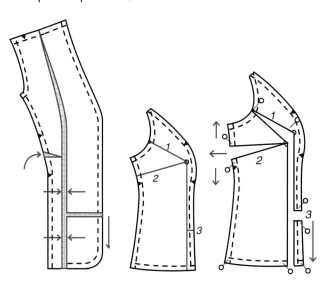

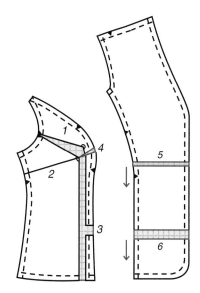

FABRIC FITTING

The Front Before

Marta again has pinned the seams on the outside so they are easier to pin to her shape. She has slipped in shoulder pads. The jacket looks great!

The Back Before

The jacket back looks good. But since her right hip is fuller than her left, we will take in the left back seam and let out the right back seam until the center back seam is straight.

pulls

The Back After

The jacket back looks good.

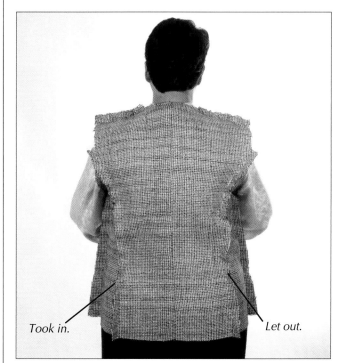

Took in. *Let out.*

THE FINISHED CARDIGAN

Marta models her new jacket. Did you notice she made many of the same alterations on both patterns?

Anastasia

The Front Before

Anastasia is Marta's daughter. She has very few alterations—being young helps! All looks good except her hips are a little fuller than the pattern's.

The Front After

We let out the side seam and the hips fit fine.

The Back Before

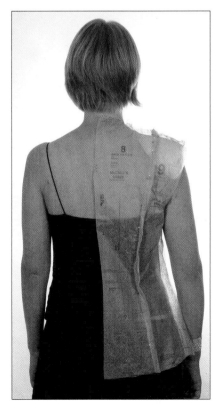

From the back you can see that the center back is not coming to her center back in the hip area. Letting out the side seam will correct this.

The Shoulder Seam Before

Anastasia has a forward shoulder.

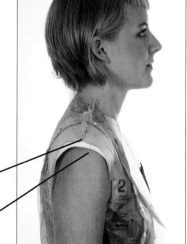

pattern shoulder

middle of arm

The Shoulder Seam After

We pivoted the shoulder seam toward the front, in line with the center of her arm. See pages 38 and 39 for how to do this alteration.

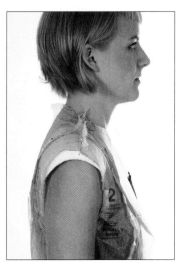

The Front in Fabric

We decided to take in the bust area—easy in a shoulder princess.

The Back in Fabric

Then we deepened the seams at the waistline for more shape.

Sleeve Length

The sleeve is pinned at the underarm only.

THE FINISHED JACKET

Anastasia in her finished embossed velvet jacket—perfect with skirts or jeans. We decided to flip back the sleeve for a fun look.

Laurie

The Front Before

The jacket center front does not come to Laurie's center front. Her bust is lower than the bust curve in this shoulder princess pattern.

The Front After

We have lowered the bust fullness to match Laurie's. We pinned the tissue center front to hers and measured the distance between the stitching lnes at the bust line so we'd know how much to add.

The Back Before

The center back stitching line is not coming to Laurie's center back.

The full bust adjustment has been made and we are ready to cut out her jacket.

NOTE: The shoulder princes alteration is similar to the armhole princess. See page 47.

The Back After

Always do a broad back alteration before you decide the amount to add for a full bust. This shows both a broad back and a high round back adjustment.

The Front in Fabric

The jacket hangs nicely. Her right hip is smaller than her left, so we took in the left side seam.

The Back in Fabric

The back looks good with the right side seam taken in.

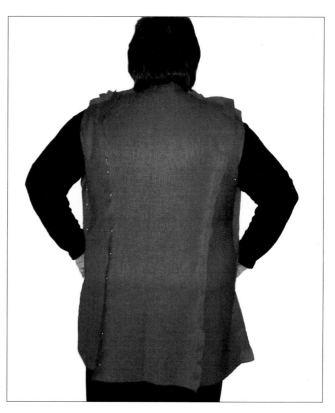

THE FINISHED JACKET

This simple zipper-front jacket is made from a polyester/rayon/ linen blend fabric by Pago called Santa Cruz. It looks like a silk suiting, but is easy-care. The jacket fits and the style flatters Laurie.

Fitting Gets Easier the More You Do It

Sue

Co-author Sue Neall is fitting a simple McCall's cardigan jacket. She measures from the jacket center front to the pin at her center front for needed bust width.

Sue takes a tuck in the neckline tapering to nothing at the armhole until the center front hangs straight.

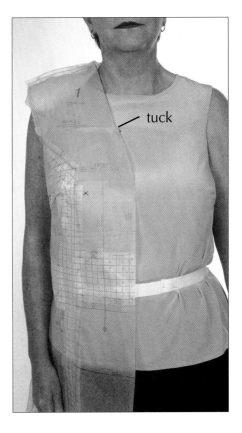

tuck

She alters for her full bust, but note that the center front is swinging toward her side.

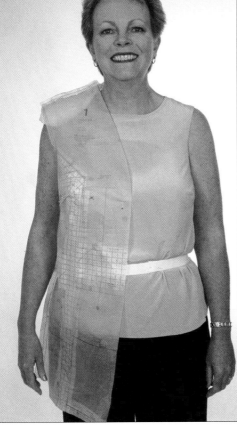

THE FINISHED JACKET

Sue in her finished zip-front cardigan with perfectly matched stripes. See page 123 for stripe techniques.

Alterations are Consistent

Now Sue fits a Vogue blazer pattern and makes the same bust adjustment she made on the McCall's cardigan on page 53. She again tucks the neckline to make the CF hang straight.

tuck

full bust alteration

In this McCall's jacket with a collar, she has to take the same neckline tuck to make the pattern hang straight in the front. She makes a tuck in the collar that matches the tuck in the jacket neckline.

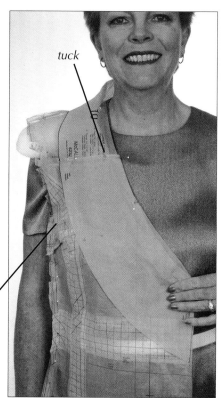

tuck

full bust alteration

Same Design—Three Different Looks

Tissue fitting allows you to see how the design looks on you before you cut it in fabric and to make changes if you desire. The three authors wear their own version of the same pattern. Marta cut hers off at the center front as she didn't want to button it. Plus, she added machine embroidery. Pati narrowed the collar a little and Sue's is just like the pattern.

CHAPTER 9

Cutting, Marking, and Interfacing

Check the Pattern
Allow for "Turn of Cloth"

If you bend a book, the back cover will slip out. The thicker the book, the more slippage you will get. This is also what happens when

one layer of fabric is folded over the other. If you make the under layer smaller, it won't do that. Make the under layer 1/8" - 1/4" (3mm-6mm)smaller, depending on the weight of the fabric.

To allow for this "turn-of-cloth," lay jacket front pattern over facing pattern and make sure the jacket is 1/8"-1/4" smaller from the top to the bottom of the roll line.

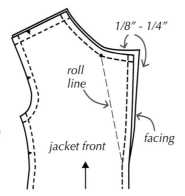

1/8" - 1/4"

roll line

jacket front

facing

Lay under collar over upper collar, matching neck edges. The outside edges of the under collar should be 1/8"-1/4" smaller.

NOTE: Some patterns are designed this way, but check to make sure.

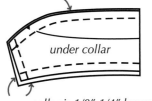

neck edges match

under collar

upper collar is 1/8"-1/4" larger

Why a Bias Under Collar?

In jackets, the under collar controls the roll of the upper collar, which is why it is cut on the bias. If it were cut in one piece, the lengthwise grain would go perpendicular to the point at one end and parallel to the point on the other end.

When it is cut in two pieces, however, and seamed at the center back, the grain is the same in both collar points.

one-piece bias under collar   *two-piece bias under collar*

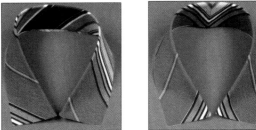

This is important for both collar points to look the same. Remember, usually the **lengthwise grain is stronger than the crosswise grain.**

Collar Grainline

On the under collar, we like the gorge line to be parallel to the lengthwise grain to prevent stretching when the collar is sewn to the bias neckline. Many patterns have the lengthwise grain marked in the opposite direction, making the gorge line parallel to the less stable crosswise grain. Redraw the grainline parallel to the gorge line.

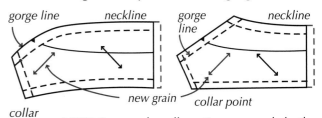

gorge line   *neckline*   *gorge line*   *neckline*

collar point   *new grain*   *collar point*

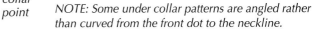

NOTE: Some under collar patterns are angled rather than curved from the front dot to the neckline.

Mark Roll Line on Jacket Front and Under Collar

If a roll line is not printed on the pattern **undercollar** and on the **front**, pin front, back and undercollar together along stitching lines and try the jacket on. Roll collar and lapel until collar covers back neckline seam and the gorge line is smooth. Crease and mark tissue along the fold. That is your roll line.

Mark roll lines on collar and lapel.

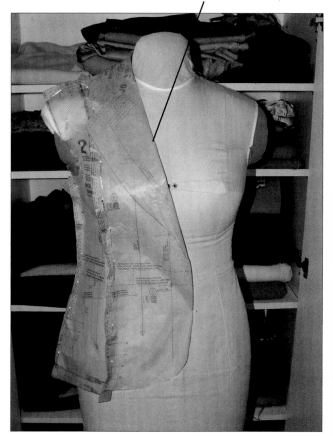

Check the Fabric Grain

Woven fabrics are made of lengthwise and crosswise yarns, which need to be perpendicular to each other. When they are, the fabric is said to be "on grain" or "squared."

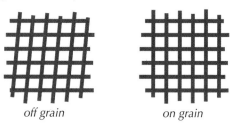

off grain   *on grain*

Find the Crosswise Grain

The lengthwise grain is parallel to the selvages (finished edges) and is usually the strongest grain. The crosswise grain runs across the fabric from selvage to selvage. It usually has a bit of give.

Tear the fabric along the crosswise grain. If it won't tear, pull on a crosswise thread and cut along it as you pull. Do this on one end of the fabric so you will have one straight-of-grain edge.

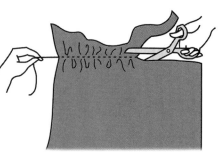

Place the fabric on a gridded surface. Fold fabric in half lengthwise, matching selvages. Line up the fold and selvages with the lines on the board.

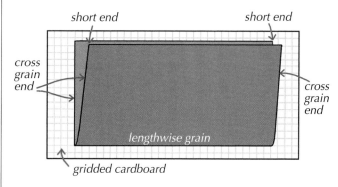

short end   *short end*

cross grain end   *cross grain end*

lengthwise grain

gridded cardboard

Straighten or "Square" the Grain

If the cross grain ends don't line up with the gridlines, pick up the short ends and pull as shown. Put the fabric back on the gridded board. Both grains should be along the grid lines. (Exception: Most denims can't be straightened.)

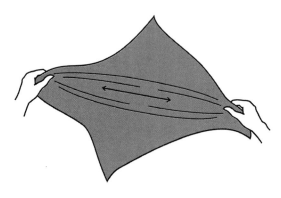

The grain of most wools can be squared by just steaming. Pin the fabric squared to a padded pressing table. Steam until all diagonal wrinkles are gone. After cooling and drying, the fabric should remain square.

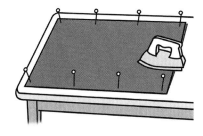

See our book *Dream Sewing Spaces* for how to make a padded pressing board. (Some people use their bed.)

TEST Fabric for Steam Shrinkage

On a padded pressing surface or a bed, you can steam dry-cleanable fabric to shrink it. Do not use an ironing board because steamed fabric draping over the edge will stretch. This fabric needs to have the wrinkles steamed out, but does it also need to be steam shrunk?

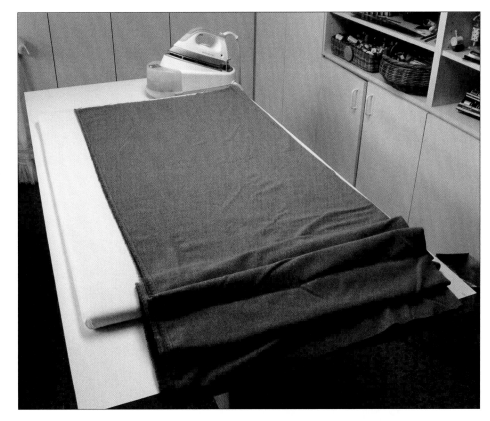

To test the fabric, place the iron in one spot on the fabric and steam for a few seconds. Then remove the iron.

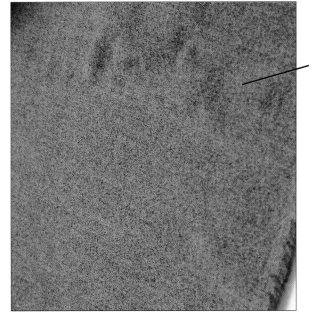

puckers around iron imprint

Puckers next to the iron imprint means the fabric will shrink with steam during construction, so you should steam it thoroughly before cutting. If it doesn't pucker, you are ready to cut. You don't need to preshrink the fabric.

Cut Fashion Fabric

◆ **Fold fabric right sides together.** Then your center back seam will be ready to sew.

◆ **Lay all pattern pieces on the fabric in one direction** using the "with nap" layout. Often it is difficult to see if there is a color difference until pieces are sewn together. Better to use a little extra fabric than risk a variation in shading or conflicting line angles on a twill weave fabric.

Both ends of the grainline are an equal distance from the edge of the fabric.

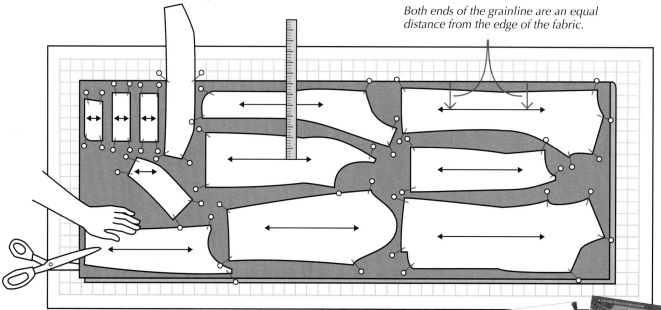

◆ **All pieces MUST be laid "on grain."**
That means that the long black arrows printed on each pattern piece MUST run parallel to the selvage or the fold. Measure from two or three points along the arrow to the selvage to ensure each measurement is the same.

◆ **Pin straight into fabric.** Save time and improve accuracy by pinning straight through the pattern and fabric and into a cardboard or padded surface. Pin only in the corners and angle the pin heads away from the center of the tissue. This prevents the tissue from scooting while cutting. Place one hand along the edge of the tissue to hold it down as you cut.

◆ **Or pin through all layers.**
Marta likes pinning through pattern and fabric because she likes to leave the pattern pinned to the fabric until she works with the piece. She pins only in the corners with pins pointing to the corners.

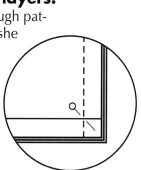

For more important sewing tips for quality garments, see *Couture, the Art of Fine Sewing* and *Mother Pletsch's Painless Sewing* .

Snip-Mark While Cutting

Accurate marking is one of the most important ways to ensure a professional looking jacket.

Marking begins during cutting. Snip-marking is very accurate. **Snip only 1/4" (6mm) into the edge of notches or where there are circles.** The circle for your size will be 5/8" from your cut edge. Do not mark darts until after applying interfacing.

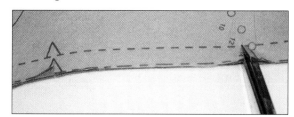

In a jacket, snip-mark all of the following:

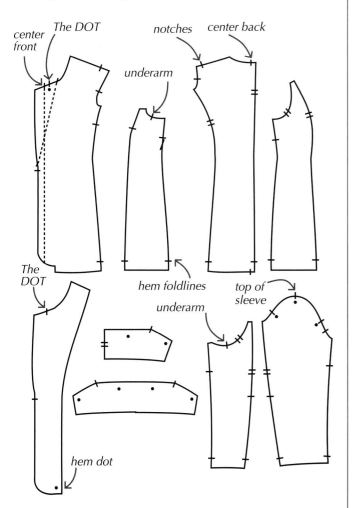

NOTE: THE DOT is at the "V" where the collar and lapel come together. You can snip it now, but you will mark it again with a pen (page 62) as accuracy is crucial.

Quick Tip

Use sticky dots instead of snip marking for ravely fabrics.

Now Cut the Lining

Make the same alterations on the lining pattern pieces that you made on the jacket pieces.

If you are using the "Quick Lining" method on page 91, cut the underarm of the front, back and sleeve 1/4" (6mm) higher to allow the lining to go up and over the sleeve underarm seam.

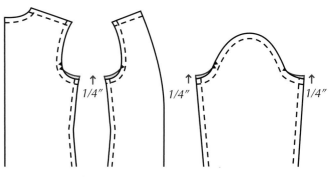

Also, make sure your pattern has a back pleat to keep the lining from tearing when you reach. If it does not, see below on how to add one.

Creating a Pattern for the Lining

If you are using a pattern that has no lining pattern pieces, you can create them. Place facing pattern pieces on jacket pattern pieces. Mark facing edge with a dotted line. Measure 1¼" from inside edge of facing toward center front for lining cutting line.

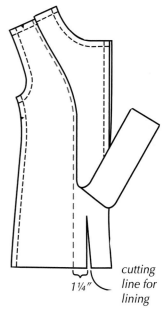

cutting line for lining

1¼"

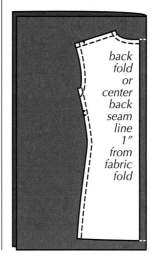

back fold or center back seam line 1" from fabric fold

If there is no back facing, use the back pattern piece as is, but add a pleat by placing the center back fold or seamline 1" (2.5cm) from the fold of the lining fabric. Use the sleeve pattern piece, eliminating any vent extensions.

Cutting Fusible Interfacing

Note that most weft interfacings have a definite crosswise thread. Don't confuse this with the lengthwise grain. The pattern grainline should be parallel to the lengthwise grain.

We like to cut the interfacings slightly smaller than the pattern so they will not accidentally fuse to the pressing surface.

Let's start with a simple upper collar:

1. Cut the long edge first, then one of the short edges.

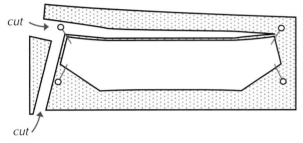

2. Slide the pattern piece about 5/8" (1.5cm) up and over long and short edges of the pattern piece you just cut. Cut remaining sides.

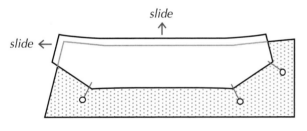

3. Re-center the pattern to see the results. VOILA! The interfacing is slightly smaller.

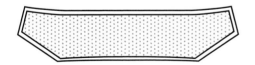

NOTE: If you like "live action," Marta shows how to cut interfacing in this video and DVD.

To cut a front interfacing slightly smaller than the fashion fabric do the following:

1. Cut front edge, neckline, and shoulder.

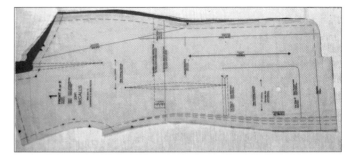

2. Slide pattern 5/8" toward cut edges. Fold up hem.

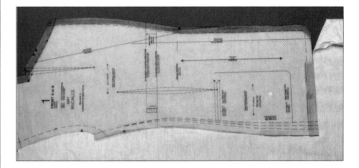

3. Now cut side and bottom.

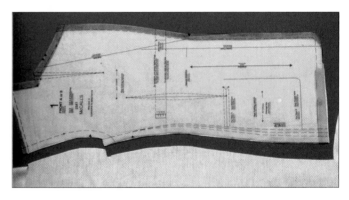

Interfacing will be slightly smaller than the pattern.

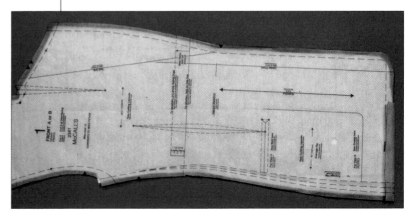

Fuse Interfacing

Read the manufacturer's directions. If they are not available, use these general directions.

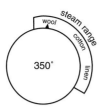

1. Set the iron to the **wool** setting.

2. Press fashion fabric from the wrong side to remove wrinkles.

3. Put the pattern on top of the fabric to be sure you have not distorted the fabric before fusing. Adjust the fabric to match the pattern.

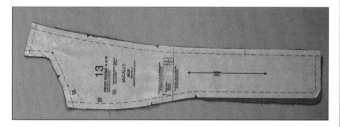

Bias easily stretches. This bias silk tweed under collar has become distorted.

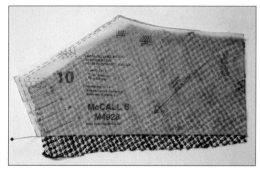

Re-shape the fabric to fit the pattern.

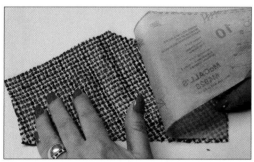

Now it matches the pattern and you are ready to fuse.

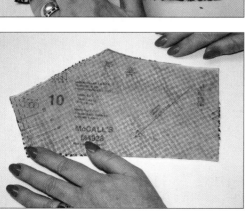

4. Use a see-through press cloth to protect the iron.

PRO Tip Mark one press cloth for using with fusible interfacings and one for pressing fabric.

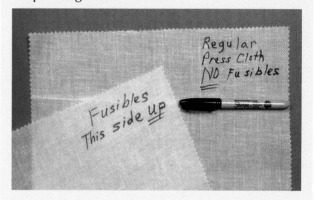

5. Place the grainy side of the interfacing on the wrong side of the fabric. Start at one end of the fabric and steam for 10-15 seconds. Move the iron ahead lapping as shown until the whole piece is fused. Some fabrics may need more time and steam than others.

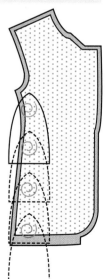

Always allow fused pieces to cool before moving them. **Don't check how well the interfacing is adhered until it is completely cool.**

If you have a steam generator iron, you may need only 8-10 seconds. **Extra steam may cause shrinkage in wool fabrics. To check for shrinkage, lay the pattern back on the interfaced fabric and mark seamlines if they are less than 5/8" (1.5cm).**

Clean your iron BEFORE fusing! Use a hot iron cleaner. Squeeze hot iron cleaner onto several layers of terry cloth. Iron on top of the cleaner firmly with a hot iron until all the residue comes off.

Mark Interfacing

You snipped the edges while cutting. Now mark darts, buttonholes, etc. A water-soluble marking pen will bleed through the tissue, leaving ink on your fabric. Test your fabric first to make sure the ink doesn't go through to the right side or become permanent. If you are worried about the ink disappearing, go over the marks lightly with a pencil.

1. Mark the darts. Clip the dart stitching lines at the edge of the fabric.

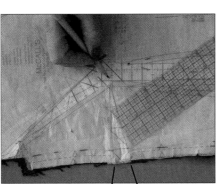

Snip dart ends.

2. Mark the neckline seams on BOTH the front and the front facing.

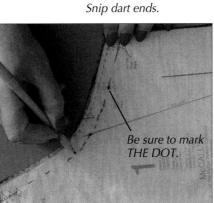

Be sure to mark THE DOT.

3. Lift the pattern and darken the marks if necessary using the same pen or a pencil.

Mark buttonhole, front edge of pocket placement, and roll line.

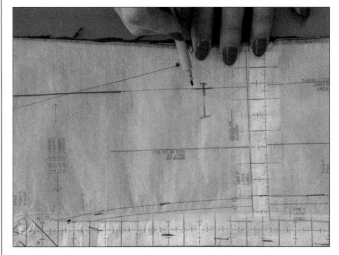

Also, make sure darts stop within the welt box.

If the dart stops short of the welt box, the welt will be more difficult to sew.

Lengthen the dart to stop between the long lines of the welt.

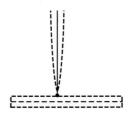 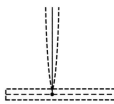

4. Remove the pattern and connect the dots to draw the roll line and the darts.

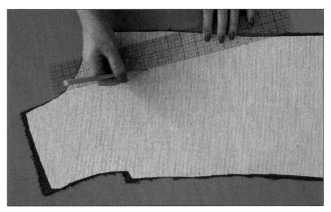

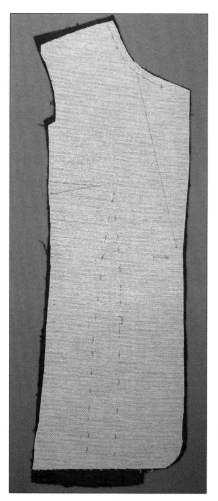

The front now has all the necessary markings.

5. Now mark the collar roll line by placing the collar pattern piece onto the fused under collar.

Mark Darts Where There Is NO Interfacing

If there are darts in the back waist or shoulder, it is best to mark them with pins as the ink might show on the right side.

Put pins through pattern dots. Remove the pattern. Put pins in the bottom layer in the same place the first pins came through. Now pin darts together. Jacket darts are often shaped, and have several marking dots.

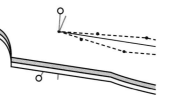

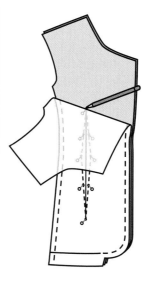

Pins falling out? Mark the pin position with a chalk pencil before removing pins.

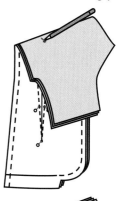

Or, use tracing paper. Be sure to test it on a scrap to make sure you can't see marks on the right side and that they wash out or steam away. Make sure the iron won't "set" them to be permanent.

NOTE: A plastic baggy on top of your pattern will keep the pattern from tearing.

PRO Tip There are times when tailor tacks are the best method of marking, such as for velvet.

◆ Use a long double-strand of thread. Sew a running stitch through the tissue and both layers of fabric making a loop at circles you are marking.

◆ Snip the middle of the loops and each stitch so you can lift off the pattern.

◆ Gently pull the layers apart and snip threads between so that some thread remains in each layer.

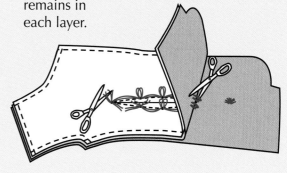

CHAPTER 10

Jacket Front

The sewing sequence for most jackets is similar. We have written this book in an order you could actually follow in sewing a jacket. We will sew a classic blazer with a side panel. Skip any techniques and details that don't apply to your style.

Our jacket is in a heavy wool. Therefore, we fused interfacing to the entire front and under collar. We also fused 1½" (3.8cm) bias strips on the hems of the back, side panel, and sleeves. We basted a sew-in poly/cotton interfacing ("back stay") across the upper back. Complete instructions for the back begin on page 76.

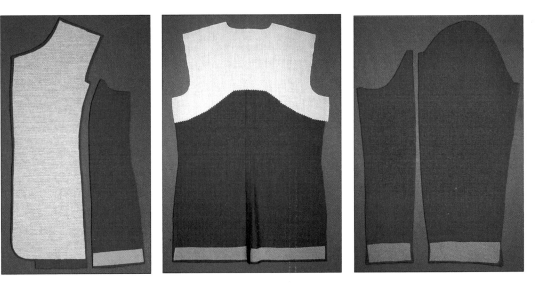

Most lighter-weight fabrics will also have a lightweight fusible or sew-in underlining on the side, back, and upper collar. Extra hem interfacing would not be needed on those pieces. The non-fusible back stay would still be basted on top of the underlined back.

After fusing and marking (Chapter 9), we like to pin the main pieces together and try on the jacket to check the fit before continuing construction.

It is especially important to check the dart positions. Darts sometimes become lower in fabric than they were in tissue.

Also, fabric may seem to have "grown" meaning you may need to take deeper seams.

If you are uneven, you can fit both sides separately.

Blazer photo courtesy of the McCall Pattern Company.

OPTIONAL: TAPE THE ROLL LINE

The lapel roll line runs on a bias grain. Fusibles stabilize the bias, so we often don't add a stabilizing tape. However, if you want to be sure there will be no stretch or if you are full busted and want to ease the roll line into your chest to prevent gapping, tape the roll line.

1. Cut 1/4" (6mm) cotton, linen, or polyester tape the length of the lapel roll line. Place tape next to the roll line and pin at lower edge.

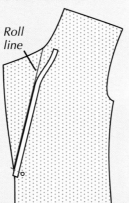

Roll line

CUSTOM TAILORING TIP:

If you want to later continue the tape into the collar roll line, cut the tape 2" (5cm) longer than the lapel roll line. (See page 79.)

2. Mark the neck seam line on the tape. Pull the tape so that the mark moves up past the seam line 1/4" (6mm) or up to 1/2" for fuller busts and long roll lines. Pin the tape in place. Evenly ease the jacket to fit the tape.

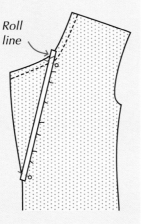

Roll line

Do both fronts at the same time so they look the same.

3. Fell stitch the tape in place. (See page 9.)

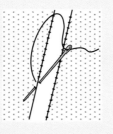

 You can machine tape the roll line. Stitch along each side of the tape, but sew the last two inches at the bottom by hand so your machine stitches won't show when the lapel rolls to the outside.

Sew and Press Darts and Seams

Sew darts in fronts. Stitch from wide end toward the point. Change to a stitch length of 1mm (18 stitches per inch) for the last 1/2". This will slow the machine, allowing you to place the last few stitches right on the edge of the fabric.

single-end dart

Avoid having to tie the threads at the dart point to secure the stitches. When the needle is off the edge, raise the needle, lift the presser foot, and pull the fabric 1/2" toward you. Then stitch in the dart fold to anchor the threads. If you plan to slash the dart open, stitch close to the dart stitching so you won't cut off the "anchor."

double-ended dart

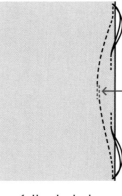

Overlap stitches.

For a double-ended dart, sew from the center to each end, overlapping a few stitches.

For bulky fabrics, carefully slash through the fold of the darts to almost 1/2" from the point. For wide darts, trim seam allowances to 1/2".

Press dart open over a ham. (See page 30-31 for pressing tips.)

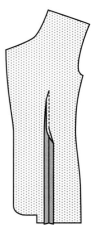

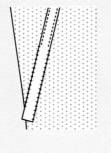

Pin and stitch side front to front. Clip seam allowances on the inside (concave) curve **only if necessary** to fit the outside (convex) curve.

Always sew with the inside curve on top. That means you will sew up on one front and down on the other. Press all seams open.

If you are sewing a jacket with princess seams see tips on page 120.

Sew Pockets to Fronts

It is easiest to sew the pockets and front details before sewing the fronts to the back. The most common pocket styles are patch and double-welt. See page 113 for more pocket options. If you plan on bound buttonholes, sew them now also.

(See page 109).

Patch Pockets - can have squared or rounded corners. They can be lined or unlined and hand sewn or machine stitched in place. You might consider a small patch pocket on the lining inside your jacket to hold your charge and identification cards.

Welt Pockets - can be double or single, straight or slanted, and with or without flaps.

Patch Pockets

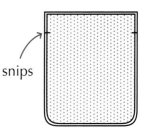

1. Fuse interfacing to the wrong side of the pocket.

snips

2. Stitch the pocket lining to the upper edge of the pocket, right sides together, machine basting for 2" (5cm) at center. (Later, clip basting to turn pocket.) Press seam allowances toward lining.

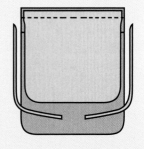

PRO Tip The lining should be 1/8" (3mm) smaller than the pocket so the lining will not show. If the pattern was not designed that way, trim 1/8" from the sides and bottom edge of the lining now.

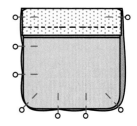

3. Fold down the pocket facing, right sides together, along the hemline (marked with snips). Make sure the fold is on the straight grain! Pull the lining to the edge of the pocket fabric and pin. Since the pocket is larger than the lining, it will look slightly "bubbly."

4. With the lining on top, stitch the sides and lower edges

PRO Tip Use small stitches (1mm) around curves. This not only reinforces curves so you can trim closely, it also slows the machine so curves will be smoother.

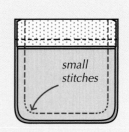

small stitches

Quick Tip

Press the lining seam allowances toward center so the pocket will have a sharper edge after turning to the right side.

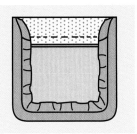

PRO Tip

BEFORE TRIMMING, make sure BOTH pockets are identical.

5. Cut corners diagonally. Trim seam allowances to 1/4" (6mm) and even closer in the curved areas. (Fusible interfacing will prevent raveling!) This usually eliminates the need to notch the curves. However, if your fabric is bulky, use pinking shears to notch the curves.

6. Clip the basting and turn pocket right side out. Press from the lining side. You will see fashion fabric around the edge if you trimmed the lining 1/8″ smaller; therefore, the lining will never show! Slipstitch opening closed.

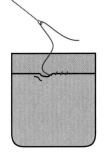

Quick Tip

Instead of slip-stitching the opening, slip a strip of fusible webbing into the opening on the wrong side and fuse the seam allowances together.

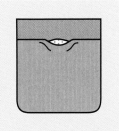

7. Pin pocket in position on each front.

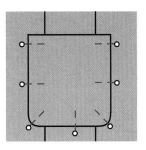

FIT Tip

If you have one hip fuller than the other, place the pockets so they are the same distance from the center front on both fronts. It won't be noticeable that there is more distance to the side seam on one side than on the other.

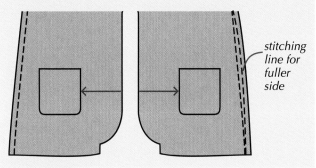

stitching line for fuller side

Quick Tip

Steam-baste pockets to jacket with fusible webbing. Place 1/4" (6mm) wide strips of webbing on wrong side of pocket edges. Holding iron 1" (2.5cm) above pocket, steam until webbing is tacky. Position pocket on jacket and fuse.

Or use Steam-A-Seam®, which is already tacky. Stick it to the pocket edge and remove the protective paper.

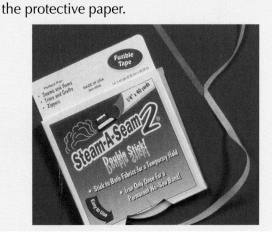

8. Check both pockets in the mirror to make sure they are at a flattering position. Double-check that both sides are identical.

Fuse one pocket in place. Place other pocket on top of it, right sides together. Stick fusible web to the edges.

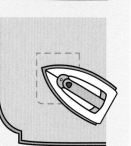

Place the other front on top matching all edges. Lightly press wrong side of second front until pocket is slightly fused in place.

VOILA! Both pockets are identically placed!

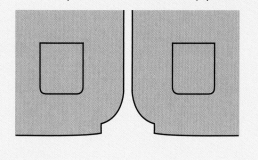

FIT Tip

If the jacket is oversized and loose-fitting, the pockets can be placed flat on the fronts. However, if the jacket is fitted, you need to fuse over a ham. This adds the same curve as your body so that the fabric under the pocket won't buckle when on your body.

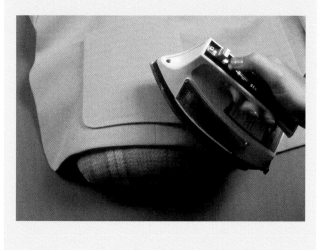

9. Edgestitch close to sides and lower edges of pocket.

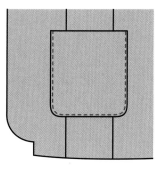

Designer Tip

Hand-sew pockets in place with a slip stitch (page 9). Fold jacket away from pocket edge and stitch through edge of pocket, then **straight down** to fold of jacket, **straight up** through edge of pocket, and so on. Pull threads until they disappear.

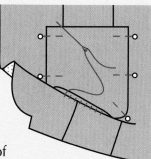

In the photo, we have used white thread. We have pulled the thread tight near the top of the pocket and the thread disappeared.

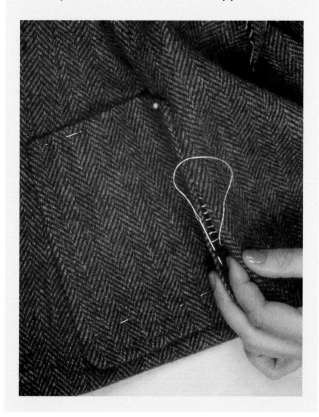

"No-Fail" Double-Welt Pocket

You may have tried a method or two during your sewing life and found welt pockets far too daunting; but although there are lots of steps, this is a NO-FAIL welt pocket! TRUST US! The key to success is accurate placement and careful stitching.

This is a double-welt pocket. You can make it straight or angled.

Slip a lined pocket flap into a welt and it becomes a traditional flapped menswear-type double-welt pocket.

Note: If the pocket is slanted, the ends are cut and sewn on the straight of grain.

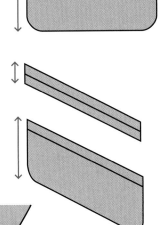

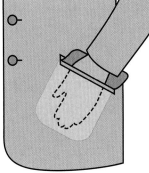

If the pocket is slanted, the lining is at the same angle.

Make a TEST Welt Pocket

There are two reasons to make a test pocket. First, you can practice the steps without working up a sweat, because it isn't on your jacket! Second, since the width of the welts depends upon the thickness of the fabric, you might need to make the basting lines a little teeny tiny narrower or wider in step 9, page 72, so they fit in the box PERFECTLY!

Prepare Pocket Pieces

The standard finished welt pocket is 5½" (14cm) long.

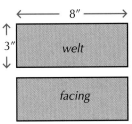

Welt - For each pocket with a flap, cut a rectangle of fashion fabric 3" (7.5cm) wide and 8" (20.5cm) long.

For each pocket without a flap, cut another welt rectangle, which will become the facing under the welt so your lining won't show.

If your fabric is lightweight or soft, interface the welt with PerfectFuse Light. To give welts even more body, you can cord them after step 18.

 With stripes and plaids, the upper rectangle that will form the welts can be cut on the bias.

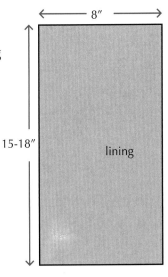

Lining - Cut a piece of lining, for the pocket bag 8"- wide and 15-18" long (38-46cm).

Stabilizer - attached to the wrong side of the jacket front under the pocket. Choose one of the following:

Pellon stabilizer - Cut a piece of Featherweight or Mid-weight Pellon (not fusible) the same size as the welt. Marta uses this non-woven stabilizer.

Perfect Fuse Sheer - Cut as above and use in place of Pellon. Sue uses this method.

Double-Welt Pocket Construction

1. **For a pocket without a flap**, pin fabric welts to both ends of the lining. (The upper one will form the welts and the lower one the facing under the welts so you won't see the lining.) **If you have a flap, use only the top welt.**

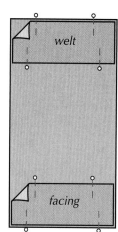

To prevent slippage when sewing, use a temporary spray adhesive. Spray wrong side of the welts. (Protect your work surface by spraying into a box or on paper.)

Stick the welt and welt facing to the ends of the lining.

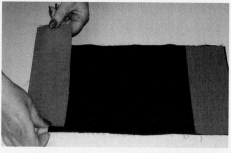

2. Pin the wrong side of the welts to the lining. Stitch welt and welt facing to lining using a straight stitch or a zigzag for ravely fabrics. Sew from the lining side unless you used the previous Quick Tip. Press on top of the stitching lines to remove puckers.

welt

welt facing

3. Mark pocket placement on the wrong side of each jacket front.

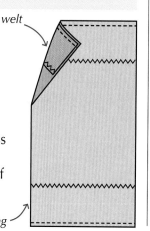
The pocket placement lines on the pattern are **only** guides. You CAN change them! If you have altered your pattern in the area of the welt pockets, the welt markings on the pattern may no longer be straight. Use the two pocket circles closest to the center front, making sure they are about 1/2" toward the center front from the dart stitching line. From those circles, draw the welt box.

Check welt placement by pinning rectangles of paper 1/2" wide by 5½" long to the right side of your jacket. Make them straight, then try them angled.

Which looks better? Do you want them higher or lower or closer or farther from the center front? Now is the time to decide.

Do you prefer straight or...

...angled welts?

4. Draw welt box on the stabilizer. **Accurate marking is the key to perfect welts.** Use a SHARP pencil to draw two parallel lines the length of the Pellon, centered, and 1/2" (1.3cm) apart.

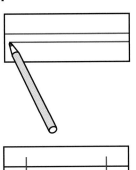

Then draw the end lines, making a 5½"-long box.

NOTE: If using a fusible stabilizer, draw the lines after fusing, step 5.

NOTE: Each welt will be half the width of the box. In this case, each welt will be 1/4" (6mm) wide. For narrower welts, draw the lines closer together.

5. On **WRONG SIDE** of the jacket, pin Pellon, matching pocket placement lines. Make sure the end of the box is NOT on a seam or dart stitching line. If it is, move it over.

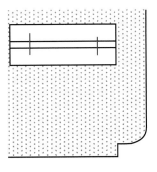

You may need to trim away part of a dart or seam allowance to remove bulk from where you are going to stitch your welt box.

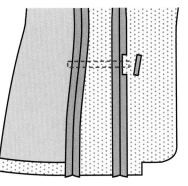

NOTE: If using a fusible stabilizer, center it over the box and fuse to the wrong side. If fusing over a seam, press lightly so it doesn't make seam imprints on the outside. Draw pocket placement lines on the interfacing AFTER fusing.

Make BOTH Fronts the Same

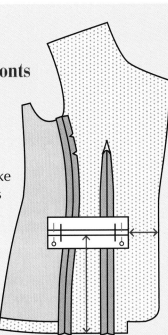

Measure the distance from the lower edge to the welt lines. Or make sure the welt ends are the same distance from the darts and front edge on both fronts.

Or, place the fronts wrong sides together. Fold one back to see if welt lines are in the same position.

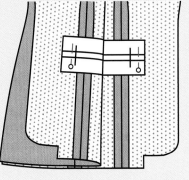

6. From the **WRONG SIDE**, stitch around the "box," using a stitch length of 2mm. (If your fabric is ravely, change to a 1mm stitch length around the corners.)

Start and stop stitching in the center of one long side of the box and overlap those stitches. NEVER start stitching at a corner! Snip threads close to fabric. READ THE NEXT TWO PRO TIPS.

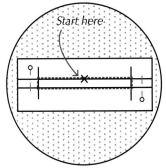

Start here

PRO Tip If you are absolutely accurate with this step, your welt pockets will be PERFECT when finished! The magic of this technique is that all the sewing is done on the wrong side, following the markings on the pocket stabilizer.

PRO Tip Turn the flywheel by hand when stitching the ends. Count the number of stitches on the first end of the box and make the same number on the other end to ensure accuracy.

Double-check markings to ensure that each side of the box is exactly the same length as its opposing side and that both pockets are placed perfectly on either side of the jacket. It is easy to make one welt pocket. The real trick is to make two, exactly the same! If they look the same now, they will look` the same when you are done!

7. From the **RIGHT SIDE**, position and pin welt end of pocket bag, centering it over the stitched box on the jacket, right sides together. Keep pins away from where you will stitch. If the grainline is obvious, make sure it is parallel to the box lines.

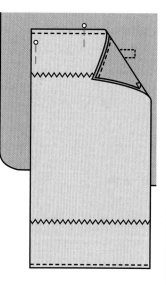

Quick Tip Fold the welt in half lengthwise, and center the fold in the middle of the box.

8. From the **WRONG SIDE**, using a stitch length of 2.5, stitch ONLY on the long sides of the box on top of the previous stitching lines. Backstitch carefully at each end by HAND TURNING the flywheel. (On computer machines, to backstitch and avoid extra stitches, hand-turn the flywheel and stitch one stitch forward and one stitch backward, then continue sewing. Practice on YOUR machine.) Clip threads closely.

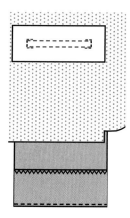

9. From the **WRONG SIDE**, stitch a row of **machine basting** (4-6 mm stitch length) 1/4" (6mm) above and another row 1/4" (6mm) below the long sides of the box, through all thicknesses. Basting rows should be longer than the box. Leave thread tails at each end of basting so removal will be easy.

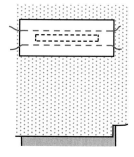

Quick Tip Use a presser foot that allows the needle to be exactly 1/4" (6mm) from the edge of the foot, (such as a quilting foot). Or draw pencil lines on the Pellon.

PRO Tip The basting lines will create the welts. Basting lines are always HALF the width of the stitched box. If the box is 1/2"-wide, each welt will be 1/4"-wide. It is important for the basting lines to be accurate so the welts won't gap or lap! Hopefully you made a TEST pocket, page 69.

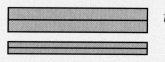

1/2" box forms 1/4" welts

1/4" box forms 1/8" welts

10. On the **RIGHT SIDE** of the garment, fold the **lower** part of the pocket lining/welt up firmly against the line of basting. Marta says NOT TO PRESS WITH AN IRON to avoid welt imprints on

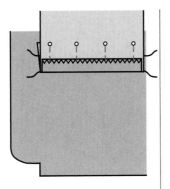

right side of THE jacket in some fabrics! Sue prefers to use an iron and PRESS VERY CARE-FULLY. Pin in place, taking a small "bite" to anchor lining/welt. You shouldn't see the pins from the wrong side of the jacket front! **Make sure the pins DO NOT extend into the area where you will be stitching.**

11. Change your machine back to a regular stitch length. From the **WRONG SIDE**, stitch again over the pre-vious stitching on the lower long side of the box, ending exactly at the corners and backstitching. You have just created the first welt!

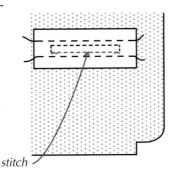

stitch

NOTE: We want to emphasize that with a **computerized machine, you may have to hand roll the reverse stitching** as sometimes the machine stitches an extra stitch or two before stopping.

 Check your welt stitching. Is it wider at one end than the other? That can happen when the welt is pinned more firmly over the basting at one end than the other. Redo the stitching now or you will be unhappy with your finished pocket.

Oops. Wider welt on this end.

12. On the **RIGHT SIDE**, pin the pocket lin-ing/welt out of the way and fold the **upper** part of the pocket lining/welt down firmly against the line of basting. Pin in place from the right side.

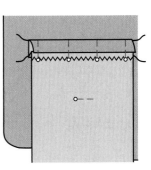

13. Flip once more to the **WRONG SIDE** and stitch on the upper line of the box. Backstitch at each end. Clip threads close to the fabric. That's welt number two.

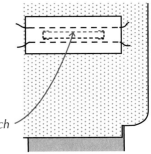

stitch

14. From the **RIGHT SIDE**, slash through ONLY the lining/weltpiece for the full length of the welt, exactly half way between the rows of stitching. DO NOT slash through the jacket yet.

Pin welts out of the way.

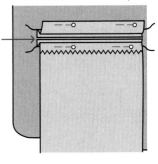

15. **Pull out the basting threads** by pulling on the bobbin thread, which generally pulls out more easily than the needle thread.

16. From **WRONG SIDE**, slash horizontally through the center of the box and diagonally into each corner CAREFULLY, using sharp-pointed scissors like tailor points. Use your fingers under-neath to make sure that you don't cut the welts.

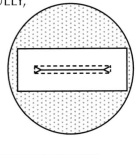

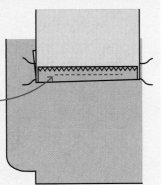

Cut right to the stitch in each corner.   Start cutting here.   *The wedge starts about 3/4" from the end.*

17. Turn the pocket lining and triangular ends to the inside, through the opening and carefully pull welts into place with your fingers. DON'T PANIC WHEN YOU LOOK AT THE POCKET FROM THE RIGHT SIDE. Gently pull the welts into line. Do this over a ham to lift the fabric and give you something to pin to.

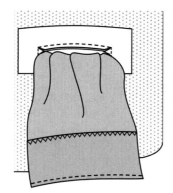

If the ends of welts overlap and look uneven...

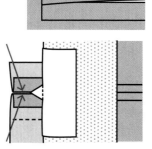

Fold the jacket back and adjust the welts until they just meet.

18. Press lightly, touching only the welt area. Let the welts cool before moving. If the welts sink into the rectangle, cord them now with heavy yarn or cord, using a bodkin or tapestry needle to pull the cording through.

 Use a press cloth to press over the pocket and steam lightly so the imprint of the pocket pieces do not show on the outside. Use your fingers to flatten the seam.

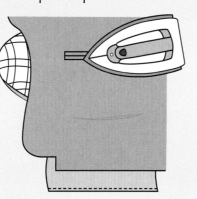

OPTIONAL POCKET FLAP: Make flap (page 75) and insert now. After making the flap, tuck it inside the welts and do the next step.

19. Catch-stitch welts together to prevent stretching during jacket construction. Stitch through welts close to seam line with a single strand of thread. Marta likes to pull the stitches until the welts slightly lap in the center to make sure they don't gap during the rest of the construction.

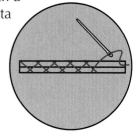

20. To finish the lining bag (with or without flaps) bring the lower edge of the lining bag up to meet the top of the upper welt. Stitch across top of upper welt, on previous stitching line.

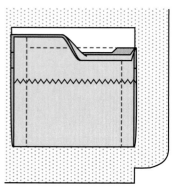

 Marta prefers to zigzag all of these layers together to flatten the bulk. Be sure you have a zigzag foot on your machine!

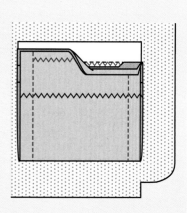

21. From the **RIGHT SIDE**, fold the jacket out of the way until you can see the triangle at the end of the box and the welts. When everything is lying flat and the welts look even in length, secure the triangles to the welts by stitching through all thicknesses exactly on top of the original box stitching. Stitch back and forth a few times to strengthen the ends.

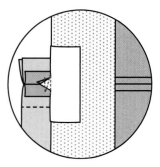

Continue stitching around the pocket through the triangle on the other side. Round off bottom of pocket bag to prevent lint from collecting in the corner. Stitching across the bottom even though it is on the fold makes this step faster and adds strength to the pocket. Press over the stitches to remove any puckers.

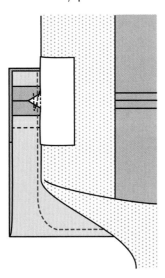

22. Trim pocket sides to 3/8″ so they are neater. DO NOT trim away the Pellon. It acts as a buffer between pocket pieces and the jacket.

Pocket Flaps

Pocket flaps do add extra bulk, so if you are hippy, you may want to avoid them. Yea! Less work!

NOTE: It is best to cut a flap after the welt opening is made so you can make sure it will fit exactly. Also, if your fabric is a plaid or has a large design, you can match the flap to the jacket front.

1. Cut one side of the flap in fashion fabric and the other in lining. This will reduce bulk.

2. Fuse lightweight fusible interfacing to wrong side of fashion fabric flap.

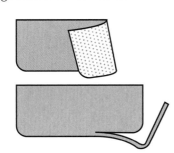

3. Cut 1/8″ (3mm) off the outer edges of the lining flap so that it will roll to the inside when the flap is complete. When you pin the smaller lining to the flap, with raw edges meeting, a "bubble" forms in the flap. When the flap is stitched and turned, however, the lining will roll to the inside and not show.

4. With the right sides together, stitch lining and flap together, around sides and lower edge, with small stitches.

5. Grade the seam allowance and trim or notch the curves.

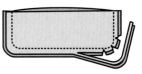

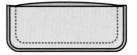

6. Turn the flaps right side out and press. Baste the raw edges together 1/4″ (6mm) from the raw edges.

Edgestitch or topstitch if desired.

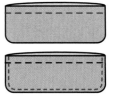

7. With right sides together, slip the flap into the welt opening, lapping the welt over the flap 1/2″ (1.3cm). Pin in place.

8. From the inside, stitch the flap to the top of the welt stitching.

9. Continue with pocket from step 19 on page 74.

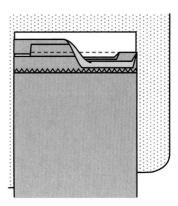

CHAPTER 11
Back and Under Collar

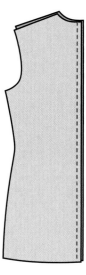

The Back Interfacing

A back stay is a layer of fabric that is loose across the upper back, but caught in the neck, shoulder, armhole, and underarm seams. It acts as a buffer between the shoulder pads and the fashion fabric. It also adds strength across the back when you reach and supports the jacket when stored on a hanger. It is used whether or not you have underlined the fashion fabric.

You can use any firmly woven sew-in interfacing such as Armo Press or a quilt cotton or muslin (homespun cotton or calico in Australia). If the fabric is a poly/cotton, just steam-shrink it. If it is 100% cotton, preshrink it.

Some patterns supply a pattern for the back stay. If your pattern does not, use the back pattern piece. Draw a line on the pattern that curves from the center back, approximately 7-8" (18-20cm) below the neck seam, to approximately 3" (8cm) below the underarm.

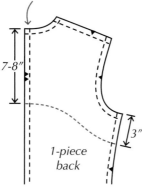

Place stitching line on fold.

7-8"

3"

1-piece back

This becomes the pattern for your stay. If the back has a center back seam, place the stitching line on the fold when cutting.

NOTE: if you have made a **very round back** alteration when tissue fitting (page 35), you will need a curved center back seam in the stay as well as in the jacket.

If your pattern has a side back panel, overlap the two pattern pieces to allow the stay to go to the side seam. This prevents the underarm from wrinkling.

Place stitching line on fold.

7-8"

3"

2-piece back

Lap pattern stitching lines.

Sew the Back

1. Stitch the center back seam of the jacket, right sides together. There should be no need to clip this seam even if it is slightly curved. Press the seam open. If you have side back pieces, sew them to the back and press seams open.

NOTE: If you have a back vent, see page 115.

2. If you have shoulder darts, stitch, slash through the fold and press open over the tailor's ham.

3. Trim the lower curved edge of the back stay with pinking shears to soften the line and prevent show through.

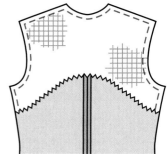

4. Place the back stay on the wrong side of the back. Make it smooth even if the edges don't exactly match.

5. Machine baste around side, armholes, shoulders, and neck. Continue construction as per the pattern instructions, treating the back and stay as one piece.

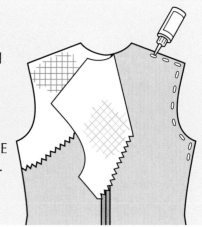

Quick Tip

Use a fabric glue and glue-baste in the seam allowances to attach the stay. DO NOT GLUE LOWER EDGE. Let dry for five minutes.

Sew the Back to the Front

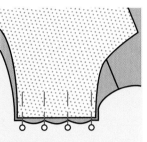 **The back shoulder** seam should be slightly longer than the front to allow ease over the shoulder blades. At the pinning and sewing stage it should be gently eased to the front.

Sew with the back on the bottom so the feed dogs will ease the back shoulder to the front. (If you have a dual-feed presser foot, disengage for this seam.)

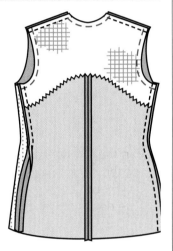

1. Stitch the back to the fronts at shoulders, right sides together.

2. Sew side seams.

3. Press the shoulder seams open over a ham to prevent shrinking out the back fullness with the iron.

4. Press side seams open over a seam roll.

5. Staystitch the neck edge of the jacket, sew from the WRONG side **exactly on the 5/8" (1.5cm) seam line** you marked on the interfacing.

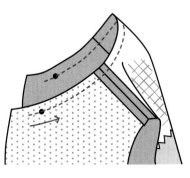

Sew Under Collar

Stitch the center back seam in the under collar, right sides together. Trim seam allowance to 1/4" (6mm) and press open.

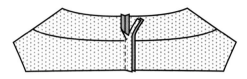

 You have already interfaced your under collar with a fusible interfacing cut on the bias. If your fabric needs more body, cut a piece of straight-grain, heavier-weight interfacing the shape of the collar stand area, which extends from the roll line to the neck edge. Fuse this piece to the under collar.

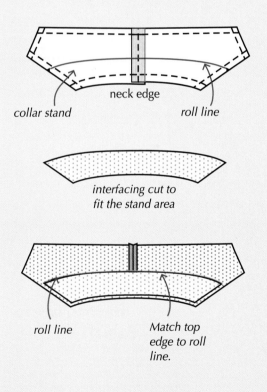

neck edge

collar stand   roll line

interfacing cut to fit the stand area

roll line   Match top edge to roll line.

To help the under collar "remember" where to roll, stitch along the roll line with a very small stitch length (1mm). As you stitch on the roll line, stretch the collar away from the roll line by pulling with both hands. This will shrink the roll line.

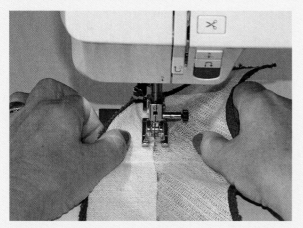

The collar will not lie flat,

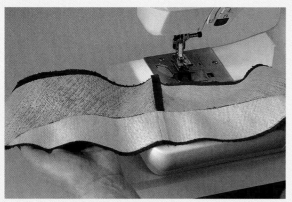

but will automatically fold on the roll line for a perfectly rolled collar.

Or, create a permanent roll in the under collar by steaming it over a pressing ham. Fold on roll line and pin to ham. Steam well. Let collar cool before moving.

Sew Under Collar to Neckline

1. Pin neck edge to under collar, right sides together, matching the collar dots first. Pin from the neckline side, not the collar side.
   NOTE: The collar dot is where the neck seam intersects the collar seam.

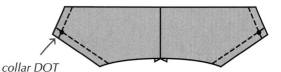

collar DOT

To make sure THE DOTS match exactly, put a pin through both dots first.

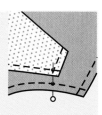

Next, pin collar and jacket at the center back. Then pin in between, matching seams and circles according to pattern. Clip the neckline as necessary to fit the under collar.

2. Stitch the collar to the neckline from the neckline side and on top of the staystitching, from THE DOT toward the center back. If necessary, pivot where the collar shape changes. At the center back, stop, then restart from the opposite DOT.

NOTE: Stitching begins at the center of THE DOT. Put the needle down in the center of THE DOT by hand. Backstitch carefully by stitching one stitch forward, then one stitch back, then sew the seam.

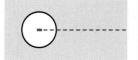

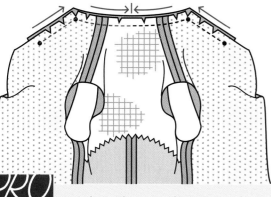

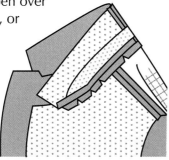 **PRO Tip** Stitching from each DOT to the center back ensures accuracy. Remember, it is easy to sew one side well. The true test is to make both sides exactly the same, which is why you marked the neckline seam on the jacket. Yes, it means the bulk of the jacket is to the right of the needle and sewing is awkward for half of the collar, but it's worth it.

3. Check to be sure the collar looks the same at both ends.

4. Trim seam allowances to 1/4" (6mm).

5. Press collar seam open over a point presser, ham, or June Tailor Board. NEVER let the jacket hang off the edge of an ironing board or you will stretch the neckline seam.

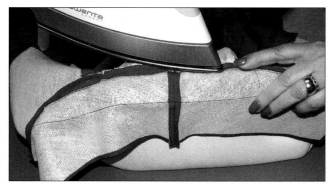

6. Stitch a row of straight stitching 1/8" (3mm) each side of the neck seam, through all thicknesses, to flatten and strengthen the seam.

Or, like Marta, center the presser foot over the neck seam and flatten it by zigzagging with a 2mm long X 3mm wide stitch.

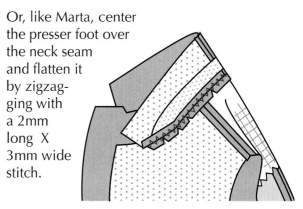

NOTE: It is OK to begin at one end and sew to the other end.

PRO Tip

If you taped the roll line and left a 2" tail for the collar, fell stitch it along the collar roll line now.

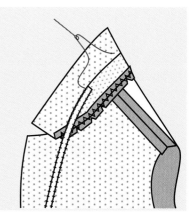

Fit Check!

Try on the jacket for a quick check of the fit before you set in the sleeves. This is the time to take in, let out, or change the shape of any of the seams.

Sleeves, Shoulder Pads, and Chest Pieces

1-Piece vs. 2-Piece Sleeves

Although you may be tempted to travel the easier path and make a one-piece sleeve, remember that in your perfect jacket the result will be disappointing. Your arm doesn't hang stiff and straight, like a soldier on parade; it bends gently at the elbow. A two-piece sleeve follows the bend of the arm and is the traditional choice in a tailored jacket. You can eliminate a vent from a 2-piece sleeve.

Sleeves with Vents

If you want a designer touch, sew a mitered sleeve vent. There is no need for frustration trying to get a professional vent finish. We will show you an EASY way!

Sleeve Length— Three Ways to Check It
(Why not try all three!)

Because the hem and vent are completed before the sleeve is set into the jacket, check the sleeve length **BEFORE** you sew the vent. **It is best to measure twice, so you'll need to cut only once!**

NOTE: Fashion variations in the sleeve cap such as gathers, pleats or tucks cause a change in the height of the sleeve cap and/or the shoulder width. Therefore, measuring the sleeve from the top to the hem is not accurate. Use the underarm measurement instead, and always fit with your shoulder pad in place as its thickness also will affect sleeve length.

◆ **Before cutting** - Measure the underarm sleeve seam and compare it to the underarm sleeve seam of a similar style jacket in your wardrobe.

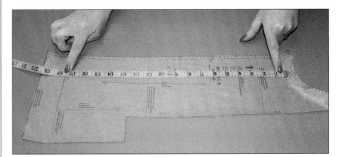

◆ **During tissue fitting** - This is a very accurate way to judge sleeve length. Pin the sleeve and jacket seams together only at the underarm.

◆ **Before mitering the vent** - Stitch unvented front sleeve seam. Pin sleeve to jacket at underarm and shoulder. Try on jacket. Wrap sleeve around wrist and make sure hem fold line is at your wrist bone. If not, move the hem fold marking until length is correct.

2-piece Sleeve with Easy Mitered Vent

Most vented sleeve patterns look like this one. To miter the vent, the upper sleeve vent extension edge should be filled in as illustrated.

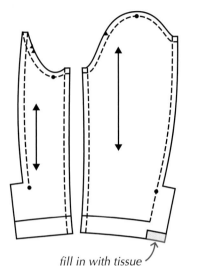

fill in with tissue

If your pattern does not have a vent allowance, add to the side back seams of upper and under sleeve pattern pieces as shown:

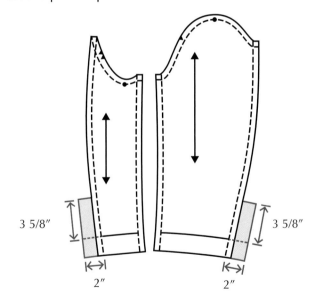

3 5/8″   3 5/8″

2″   2″

 Quick Tip Did you know that one notch in the armhole always indicates the sleeve front and two notches always indicates the sleeve back?

After cutting the sleeves, snip the following:

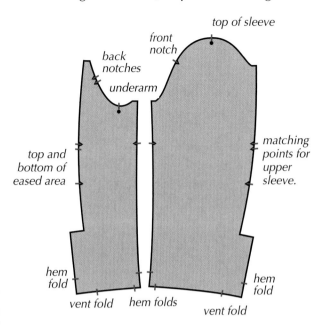

top of sleeve
front notch
back notches
underarm
top and bottom of eased area
matching points for upper sleeve.
hem fold
hem fold
vent fold   *hem folds*   *vent fold*

The vent on the upper sleeve is usually mitered for a clean finish. The under vent is not mitered.

1. Interface the sleeve hem and vent extension with a bias strip of fusible interfacing 1/4" (6mm) wider than the hem allowance. Fuse strips to hem and to upper sleeve vent extension, with the 1/4″ (6mm) extending into the sleeve past the hemline fold.

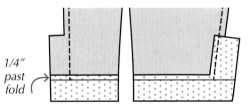

1/4″ past fold

NOTE: The interfacing is bias so it will roll softly around your wrist. Having 1/4″ extend past the hem fold softens the fold and helps it wear better.

2. Sew and press open the side front seam. Trim seam in hem area to 1/4″ (6mm) to reduce bulk.

NOTE: For clarity, the mitering art on page 82 will not show hem interfacing.

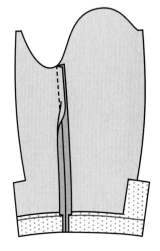

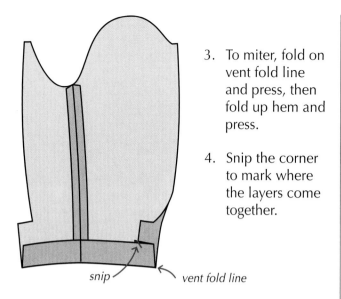

3. To miter, fold on vent fold line and press, then fold up hem and press.

4. Snip the corner to mark where the layers come together.

snip   *vent fold line*

We noticed that Marta and Pati snip the vent stitching line differently. It is interesting how people think.

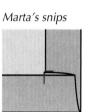

Marta's snips   *Pati's snip*

5. Unfold and draw a line connecting the snips and the corner intersection of hem and vent foldlines.

snip
corner
snip

6. Turn right sides together, match snips, and pin. On the under vent, fold up the sleeve hem right sides together and pin the side edges.

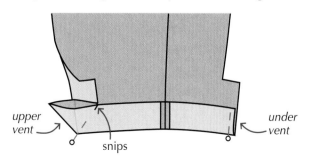

upper vent   *under vent*

snips

7. Stitch upper vent seam from snips to corner. Also, sew a 1/4" seam on the under vent while you are at the machine.

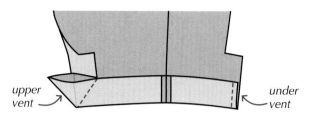

upper vent   *under vent*

8. Trim upper vent seam to 1/4". Slash bulk from corners of both sides of vent. Press seams open before turning.

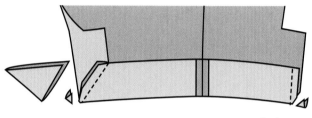

slash corner

NOTE: In fine ready-mades in lightweight fabrics, this seam is left untrimmed to allow for alterations.

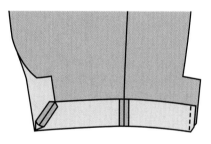

9. Turn to the right side. Push corners out gently with a point turner and press again.

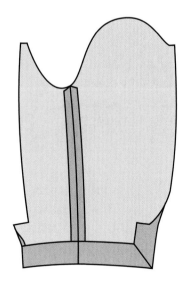

10. Hand stitch hem with blind hem stitch.

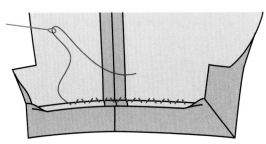

 Marta prefers to simply leave it unstitched until she sews the lining to the sleeve hem.

11. Pin remaining back sleeve seam, matching snips. The upper sleeve will be larger between snips. Add a couple of pins between the snips to even out the ease.

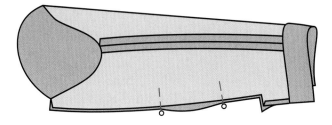

12. Sew with the larger side down and the feed dogs will help ease the excess into the under sleeve. Backstitch at the top of the vent. Then press the seam as sewn on top of the stitches to smooth the ease. It will usually disappear completely.

13. Press seam open over a seam roll. Clip into sleeve seam allowance to seam line or see PRO Tip on this page.

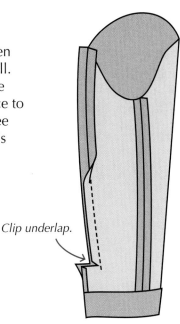

Clip underlap.

14. Press vent toward upper sleeve. You will anchor all layers with buttons.

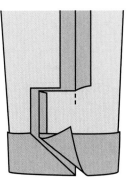

 If your fabric is not too thick or is ravely like crepe or tweed, simply press seam over at underlap rather than clipping seam and weakening it.

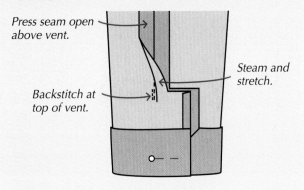

Press seam open above vent.

Backstitch at top of vent.

Steam and stretch.

Buttons on Sleeve Vents

Sew buttons into position on each sleeve, through all thicknesses.

Marta's Button Theory: If they come two to a card, she does two on each sleeve; if three to a card, then three on each sleeve!

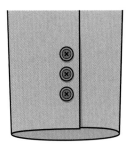

NOTE: Luxury designer lines often have working buttonholes in the vents. If you add this designer touch, stitch bound or machine buttonholes on the vent overlap before stitching the buttons in place on the vent underlap.

Sleeves without Vents

To sew a one- or two-piece sleeve without a vent, sew the seams and press them open and pin hem in place. You will sew the hem when you attach the lining.

Setting in the Sleeve with a Sleeve Head—Two Ways

METHOD I, THE "QUICK METHOD"— A BRIEF OVERVIEW

Marta first discovered this 2-in-1 QUICK METHOD in the 1970s, using a loosely woven men's tie interfacing as a sure-fire way to set in a sleeve in hard-to-ease Ultrasuede. A sleeve head is used to fill out the ease area of a sleeve cap or "head." In this method, you sew in the sleeve head BEFORE setting in the sleeve.

Purchase 1/4 yd. (25cm) of Armo-Rite or take apart an old tie! You can also use linen or loosely woven wool. Cut one **bias** strip 10-12" (30cm) long and 1½" (4cm) wide for each sleeve. (See page 118 for how to cut bias.)

Place the strip on the wrong side of the sleeve cap at the ease point notch.

Lower the needle in the 5/8" (1.5cm) stitching line. Using a 4mm stitch length, start sewing.

Begin to pull on the bias strip firmly while stitching. It will get narrower as you stretch it so that it will be about 1/4" (6mm) from the edge of the cap. That is fine as you want a smaller amount in the seam allowance and a longer amount hanging down into the sleeve.

As you sew, make sure the edge of the cap stays next to your 5/8" marking on the machine.

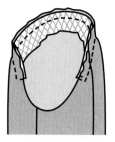

The sleeve cap is automatically eased and ready to sew into the armhole.

If it seems awkward the first time, simply unstitch and redo. With a bit of practice, it will be easy.

A FEW MORE TIPS FOR THIS METHOD

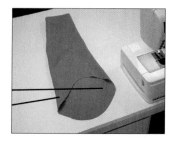

The area you will ease is the upper half of the sleeve cap.

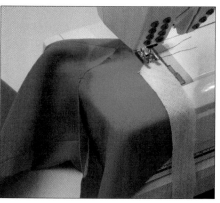

Lower needle into bias strip, which is even with edge of sleeve. Begin stitching with a 4mm stitch length.

Then pull firmly on bias strip. It narrows so is now about 1/4" from the edge of the cap.

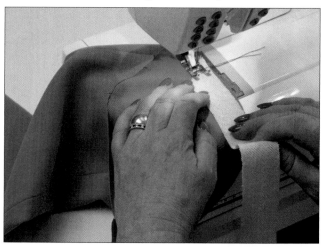

The sleeve cap is slightly gathered.

Even if sleeve is still a bit large for the arm-hole, the additional fullness will ease in smoothly.

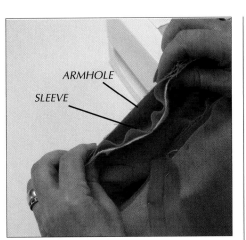

Pin the sleeve cap to the arm-hole over the curve of your hand with the sleeve on top. This will help it ease in evenly.

The bias strip helps fill in the areas that would normally want to pucker.

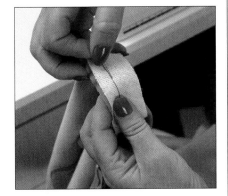

Machine baste from the bias strip side. Use your fingers to smooth out the ease as you go.

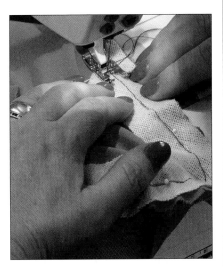

The cap is pucker-free. Always push the seam allowances toward the sleeve. See page 88 for more tips on setting in sleeves.

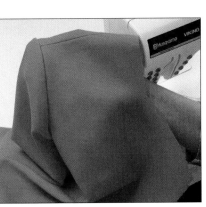

METHOD II, THE TRADITIONAL METHOD FOR SETTING IN A SLEEVE WITH A SLEEVE HEAD

This is the traditional way to set in a sleeve. If you can't find the tie interfacing for the first QUICK METHOD, use this one. You will set in the sleeve first, THEN sew in the sleeve head.

1. Machine baste (stitch length 4) two rows of stitching from notch to notch over the sleeve cap at 5/8" (1.5cm) from the edge and again 1/4" (6mm) away, in the seam allowance.

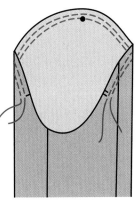

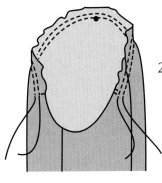

2. Pull up both rows equally.

3. Pin sleeves into jacket, matching all markings. Pin from the sleeve side with the first pin at the underarm seam or marking. Then pin at the notches and top of sleeve.

PRO Tip Marta pins in the sleeve with pins in the seam line parallel to the edge. Hold so sleeve is on top and adjust the ease as you pin. You can actually try on the pinned-in sleeve! Then as you stitch, use your fingers to smooth the ease as you remove the pins.

Always set in a sleeve with the ease facing you so you can control it.

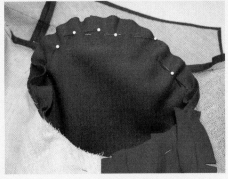

4. Machine baste (SL 4mm) sleeve to jacket.

 Try on jacket over the weight clothing you will wear under the jacket. Lap center fronts and pin. Slip shoulder pads under jacket. Pin in place. Check if the sleeves are smooth and hanging properly. If there are puckers or pulls, clip the basting and readjust fullness. See page 88.

5. Permanently stitch sleeve and reinforce stitch 1/4" (6mm) from the seamline in the underarm area only.

6. Trim to 1/4" (6mm) in underarm area only.

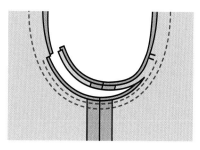

7. Press the seam allowance to get rid of the ripples. You can steam them away.

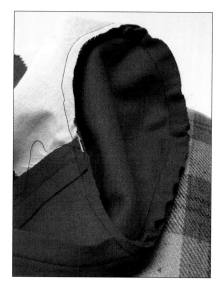

Press only the sleeve cap seam allowance from the inside to shrink away the fullness. (DO NOT top-press the cap.)

Where we pressed is now totally flat.

Continue pressing the rest of the cap seam allowance.

NOW ADD THE SLEEVE HEAD

A sleeve head is used to fill out the ease area of a sleeve cap or "head." In this method, you sew in the sleeve head AFTER setting in the sleeve.

Pin a strip of lightweight polyester fleece 2" (3.5cm) wide by 12" (30cm) long from notch to notch over the stitching on the sleeve side, with about 3/4" (2cm) over the seam allowance and 1¼" (3.2cm) into the cap. Stitch on the seam line from the garment side, through all layers. Finger press the strip toward the sleeve to fill out the cap.

 When you sew a straight strip of polyester fleece to the cap, it ripples inside the sleeve. You can sometimes see these ripples on the outside. To avoid this, substitute a 4" x 12" (10cm-30.5cm) rectangle of polyester fleece. Pin it centered to the top of the sleeve. Smooth it to fit inside the cap. Pin to cap seam.

Stitch with a 3mm stitch length EXACTLY on top of the sleeve seam through all layers. This ensures the fleece will fill in the sleeve cap.

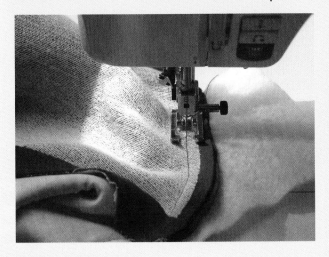

Trim the excess fleece "seam allowance" to match the sleeve seam allowance.

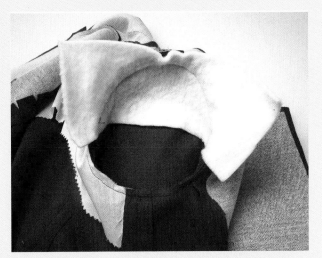

For the fleece inside the sleeve, you can leave the full width as a cap interfacing or trim as shown below.

DON'T PANIC!! From the right side, the sleeve will look like this initially.

Push the sleeve seam and sleeve head out into the cap. The shoulder pad will hold them in place.

More on Sleeve Fit

With METHOD I, these adjustments are made after the sleeve is set in. With METHOD II, these adjustments should be made BEFORE the sleeve head is added.

Fullness in the Wrong Place

Clip basting from the outside and in the cap area pull seam apart. Rotate sleeve cap until pulls disappear. Since we have been doing the forward shoulder alteration and matching the dot at the top of the sleeve to the new shoulder seam, we have not had to rotate many sleeves.

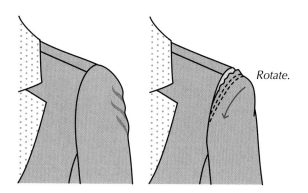

Rotate.

Sleeve Cap Too Short

To eliminate diagonal pulls, add height to the cap.

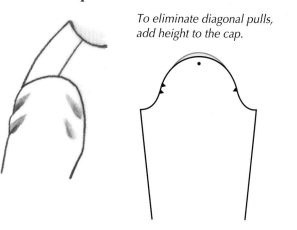

Puckers

You can ease a sleeve cap that is 1" larger than the armhole in any fabric. In some fabrics you can even ease in 2" without puckers. Patterns generally allow 1½" ease in set-in sleeves and 0-½" in shirt sleeves. The higher the cap, the more ease.

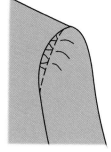

If you see puckers, BEFORE PANICKING, push the sleeve seam allowance into the sleeve. This will usually make them disappear. Check from the outside to see if the sleeve is puckered. If it is, try one or more of the following cheats! The secret to any sleeve is knowing when and how to cheat! The time to do so is after basting the sleeve into the armhole.

- Check to make sure the seam is sewn **straight**! "Wiggly" stitching can cause puckers.

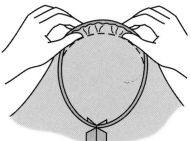

- Smooth the seam with your thumb and fore-finger. Since the basting is loose, you can often smooth away puckers.

- If puckers remain, clip your basting and re-stitch. Sometimes the second time is a charm. Always stitch on the sleeve side and use your fingers to manipulate the ease as you sew.

- If you can't get rid of the puckers, remove the stitching in the upper two-thirds of the cap. Slip the cap 1/4" farther into the armhole. Machine baste again at the **garment's** original 5/8" stitching line. If the cap still puckers, slip it in another 1/8" and stitch again.

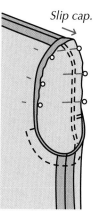

Slip cap.

Shoulder Pads

We love shoulder pads, especially raglan. Depending on fashion, they will be very thick or just "essence" of a pad. We feel jackets should always have padded shoulders to have a beautiful tailored look.

When the pattern calls for a 3/4" pad, the shoulder has been squared only 3/8"-1/2" since most pads will compact. A pad labeled as 1"-thick often measures only 1/2"-thick.

Try on the jacket and position the shoulder pads. The pads should extend past the sleeve stitching line and into the sleeves about 3/8"-1/2" (1cm to 1.3cm).

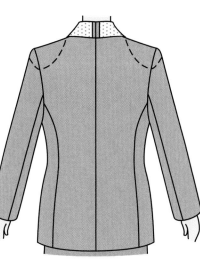

raglan pad

Pin in place from the outside.

From the right side, sew shoulder pads in place by stitching in the well of the shoulder and armhole seams using a running backstitch to catch the shoulder pad.

Hand-stitch through seam.

Our Favorite Shoulder Pad Tips

◆ When you plan to wear shoulder pads in the garment you are making, always tissue-fit with them in place or your sleeves will end up too short when you add the pads later.

no shoulder pad   shoulder pad

shorter sleeve

◆ If your bra straps make your shoulders lumpy, shoulder pads will smooth them out.

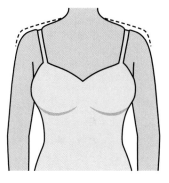

◆ We prefer raglan pads as they can be adjusted to change your shoulders when desired.

Widen narrow shoulders to balance wider hips. You can extend pads out as much as 3/4".

Extending the pads will camouflage full upper arms.

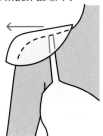 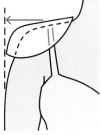

◆ You can change the slope of your shoulders or make uneven shoulders even.

If you slope a lot, use a thicker pad.

If you are very square, use a thin pad.

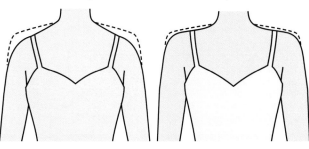

◆ If your shoulders are uneven, use uncovered, layered, molded polyester pads. Peel out layers to customize shoulder thickness.

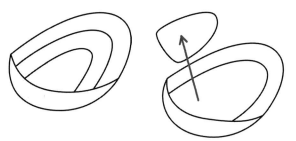

Or add layers of fleece or quilt batting to the top of one pad.

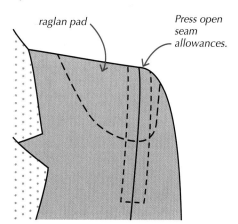

◆ Raglan pads also allow you to press the upper sleeve seam allowance open for that flat-cap look.

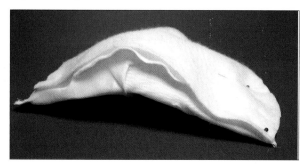

raglan pad

Press open seam allowances.

◆ To cover pads for unlined jackets, fuse a knit interfacing to the top and bottom of the pad, stretching to fit. Serge the outside edges together. Or, for a non-slippery cover, use swimsuit bra lining and stretch it around the pad. Pin and serge around the edges.

NOTE: A good current shoulder pad source is Things Japanese (USA) and Tessuti (Australia).

A Chest Piece Fills in the Front

Do you have a hollow upper chest? If you do, your jackets will dimple in that area. Add a layer or two of polyester fleece in the upper chest of your jacket.

1. Cut fleece to fit the pattern from shoulder to underarm to roll line. Cut each additional layer 1/2″ smaller than the one beneath, as shown below.

2. Place the first layer next to the armhole edge and to the roll line and shoulder seam line. Place the second layer at the armhole stitching line and 1/2″ from the first layer on all other edges.

3. Tailor baste (page 9) the layers together.

4. After the sleeve has been set in, catch chest piece to the shoulder and armhole seams.

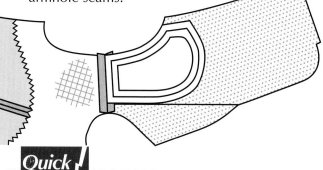

Quick Tip As an alternative to the above, simply attach a layer of fleece to the front edge of your shoulder pad as a chest filler. Extend the piece over the pad if you need to raise a low shoulder to match the other side.

CHAPTER 13

Facing, Lining, Upper Collar, and Hems

Why Line?

Lining a garment will not only make it feel luxurious and more comfortable, it will help prevent wrinkling, make it slip on more easily, and hide interfacings and inner construction.

A good lining pattern will always allow for a movement pleat at the center back and extra length to form a "jump" hem at the sleeve and jacket hems. See page 25 for suggestions for lining fabrics. Some jacket patterns have a back facing, but we like the lining to go to the neck edge in case our fabric is scratchy. See page 59 for lining cutting tips.

Be sure to make the same alterations on facing and lining pieces that you made on the jacket.

"Quick Lining"

"Quick-lining is when you sew the lining, facing, and upper collar together, then sew this unit to the jacket body. VOILA! The jacket is finished AND lined!

 Quick Tip We prefer to sew the lining pieces together while we are sewing the jacket. Then it's done when you are ready to add the facing and upper collar.

Sew Front Lining to Facing

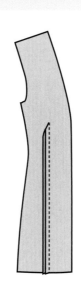

1. If there are darts, stitch them in each front. Press dart toward side seams.

2. Pin front facing to front lining, right sides together, matching notches, and clipping inside curves as necessary to fit outside curves. Stitch, **ending stitching 3" (7.5cm) from lower edge**. Press seam allowances toward lining.

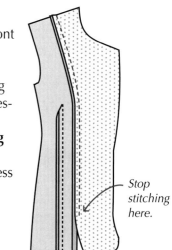

Stop stitching here.

 Designer Tip Before stitching facing to lining, add a custom touch to the inside of your jacket with preshrunk piping or decorative trim. Pin it to facing seam line and stitch in place with zipper foot. Then stitch lining to facing with facing on top so you can follow the piping stitching. See Chapter 18, Finishing Touches.

3. Stitch side front lining to front. Press seams toward front lining piece.

 **PRO Tip** It is very important to first press the lining seams flat, over the stitches, to remove puckers.

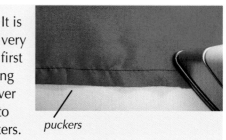

puckers

NOTE: Save time by pressing lining seams to one side rather than open. The seams will be smoother when pressed flat. Marta does this from the right side of the lining to save another step. It is not necessary to serge or finish lining seams unless you plan to wash the jacket.

Sew Pleat in Back

1. To make the pleat in the back lining, fold the back in half, right sides together, and press. Stitch with a regular stitch length where you see a solid line in the art.

   Backstitch and change to basting where you see dashed lines in the art.

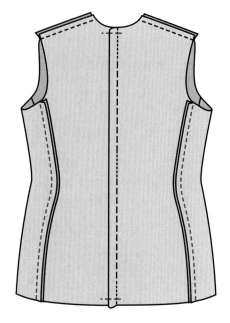

3″ - 4″
Backstitch.
Baste.
Backstitch.
2″
Backstitch.
Baste.
Backstitch.
2″

2. Press the pleat to one side. Baste across upper and lower edges to hold pleat in place.

3. Stitch back to side back. Press seams flat towards the back.

NOTE: If your pattern has a back neck facing, you need to staystitch the upper edge of the back lining and sew it to the neck facing, clipping lining as necessary to fit.

Sew Back to Front

1. Stitch the front to the back at the shoulders.

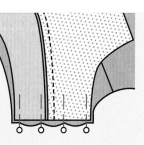

PRO Tip The back shoulder seam should be slightly longer than the front and at the pinning and sewing stage should be gently eased to retain the subtle fullness. Sew with the back on the bottom so the feed dogs will ease the back shoulder to the front. (If you have a dual-feed presser foot, disengage for this seam.)

2. Sew side or side back seams. Press toward the back.

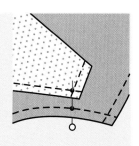

Sew Upper Collar to Lining/Facing Unit

1. Staystitch neck of lining/facing unit exactly on the 5/8″ (1.5cm) seamline.

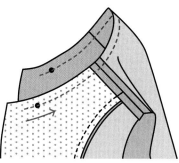

2. Pin neck edge to the upper collar, right sides together, matching the collar dots first. Pin on the neck side along staystitching. Then pin the center back and other matching points. Clip the neckline as necessary to fit the upper collar.

PRO Tip To make sure THE DOTS match exactly, put a pin through both dots first.

3. Stitch from lining/facing side on top of staystitching from THE DOTS toward the center back on both sides. If necessary, pivot where the collar changes shape. (Having marked THE DOT with a pencil first helps a lot!)

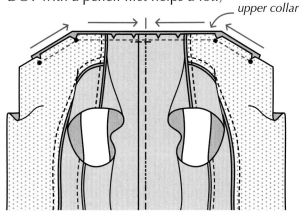

upper collar

Backstitch carefully beginning in the center of THE DOT. Stitch one stitch forward, then one stitch back, then sew the seam. This seam MUST be accurate for the collar to fit correctly.

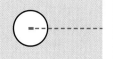

4. Trim seam allowances to 3/8" (1cm) from stitching.

 Tip Always stitching from each DOT to the center back ensures perfect accuracy. Yes, it means the bulk of the lining is to the right of the needle and sewing is awkward for half of the collar, but it's worth it.

5. Press seam open over the June Tailor Board or ham.

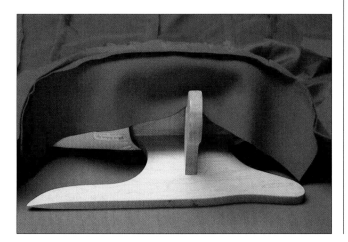

Sew The Sleeve Lining

1. For a two-piece sleeve, pin the back sleeve seam, matching snips. The upper sleeve will be larger between the snips. Add a couple of pins between the snips to even out the ease.

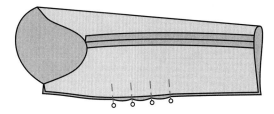

2. Sew the sleeve lining with the larger side down and the feed dogs will help ease the excess into the under sleeve. Then press over the seam to smooth the ease. It will usually disappear.

3. Press seam allowances towards the under sleeve.

Quick Tip If you want to finish jacket TOTALLY by machine, leave an 8" opening in one sleeve seam. See page 105. OR, machine baste the 8" opening closed and clip open later. Then you can press the seams, making hand-sewing the opening closed again easier.

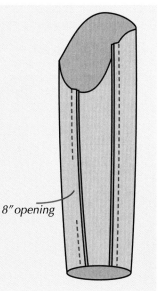

8" opening

Set in the Lining Sleeves

NOTE: Go to page 100 if you want to sew the sleeve lining by hand.

1. Machine baste two rows of stitching from notch to notch over the sleeve cap using a stitch length of 4mm. Place one row on the 5/8" (1.5cm) seam allowance and the second 1/4" (6mm) away, in the seam allowance. Pull up both rows equally.

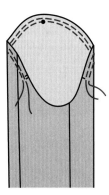

 Quick Tip Marta cheats and uses a 3.5mm stitch length which puckers a bit while sewing, helping add to the ease. Therefore, she is able to use only one row of stitching successfully.

2. With right sides together, stitch the sleeve lining into the armhole. If you did not add to the underarm area when cutting as shown on page 59, sew a 3/8″ underarm seam so the lining has room to sit above the sleeve underarm seam.

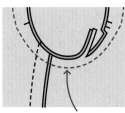

Trim to 1/4″.

3. Press seam allowances toward sleeve and trim the entire seam allowance to 1/4".

You now have completed the jacket body and lining sections, both with collar and sleeves. All that is left to do is THE SEAM!

 The DOT and The SEAM

THE SEAM is the outside edge of the jacket. There are many tricks to making this edge look professional.

THE DOT is the 4-point closure where the collar and lapel meet, forming a "V". It is the most common place to spot a homemade sign. Many people avoid making jackets for fear of how the notch will look! Fear not!

RULES:

◆ Always sew away from THE DOT.

◆ NEVER sew over THE DOT.

◆ Leaving a tiny hole at THE DOT will ensure here will be no puckers where these four seams come together. See page 96. After the lapel and collar are pressed, the hole will disappear. Better to have THE HOLE instead of THE PUCKER!

 Before sewing the outside seam, Pati likes to compare the upper collar facing unit with the jacket to make sure things are looking good. She hangs them on a hanger together. On occasion she has found the facing to be longer than the jacket. This allowed her to trim them to match **before** sewing that final seam.

Sew the Outside Seam

1. Pin the lining/facing section to the jacket right sides together. You will be sewing the collar from THE DOT to the center back, and facings from THE DOT to the bottom on each side

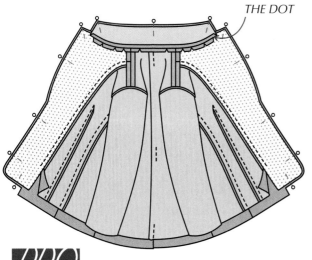

THE DOT

Make a "Tailor's Blister" to pinch out the excess fabric in the upper collar and the upper lapel points, which have been cut larger to allow for "turn of the cloth." (See page 55.) Pin a small tuck about 1/2" from the point. Remove the pins after the outer seam has been stitched.

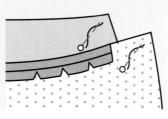

Susan's favorite sure-fire tip for a perfect 4-point closure is to take a hand needle threaded with matching thread. Tie the circles or "THE DOTS" together by picking up the last machine stitch of the upper collar and facing and the last machine stitch of the under collar and garment.

Remove the needle and simply, securely, tie the four seam allowances together. This area can no longer move. If you carefully lower the machine needle into the last stitch (at the dot) you will automatically go through the exact stitch on the other side.

Tie thread ends together.

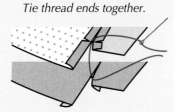

2. Stitch outer edges together. Use a stitch length of 1mm (20 stitches per inch) at all corners and curves where close trimming is required. Move the lapel seam allowances out of the way. Lower the needle into the last stitch and sew from THE DOT to the center back on each side. Backstitch carefully at THE DOT. If you have a computer machine, use the hand wheel to stitch exactly one stitch forward, one back, and then continue.

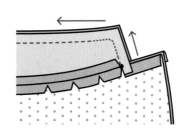

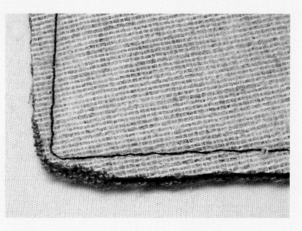
To prevent dimpling on collar points, change to a short stitch length about 1/2" from the point. Stitch two small stitches across the point. Slash at an angle from each side of the point. Fusible interfacing prevents raveling, so don't be afraid to trim closely.

3. Move all seam allowances toward the collar. Lower the needle into the last stitch and sew from THE DOT to the bottom of jacket. At the lower edge, stop stitching at THE HEM DOT, page 101. With this method you will never stitch over THE COLLAR DOT and cause puckering. It may be necessary to ease the front facing to the jacket front. A "tailor's blister" in the lapel will help. See Pro Tip on this page.

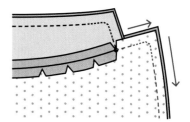

You want your notch to look like this,

not "scooped" like this.

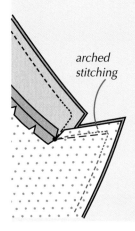

arched stitching

Stitch the top area of the lapel just slightly above the stitching line. After it is turned right side out, it will not "dimple" or curve down. This trick is especially helpful with a "peaked" collar often seen on double-breasted jackets. It may be helpful to first draw the stitching line with chalk or a pencil.

It is OK to have THE HOLE! After the lapel and collar are pressed, the hole will disappear. Better to have THE HOLE than THE PUCKER!

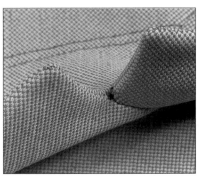

4. Once all seams are sewn, check to make sure that both sides are exactly the same.

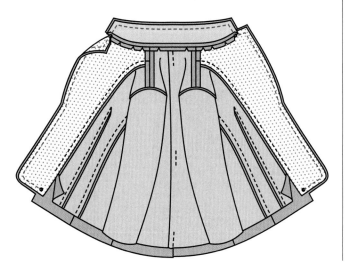

5. Trim and grade all seam allowances. Fusible interfacings prevent raveling so if you used them, you can trim closer than normal.

WHY GRADE? You'll get fewer ridges along the seamed edges. The wider seam allowance cushions the narrower one.

RULE: The longest seam allowance is always next to the outside.

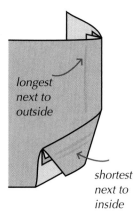

longest next to outside

shortest next to inside

Quick Tip

Trim and grade in one step by holding scissors almost flat while cutting. This is called "beveling." The top layer will end up shorter than the bottom layer, especially with heavy fabrics.

6. Outside corners may need to be notched because the seam allowance needs to fit inside the stitching line, a smaller area, when turned. Notching makes room for the seam allowance to fit.

Notch outside seam.

It will now fit when turned to the inside.

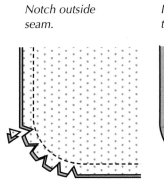

Pinking is a way to notch a curve evenly. However, with fusible interfacings, you can simply trim to 1/8" as fusibles will prevent the seam from raveling.

7. To remove bulk at corners, clip across point. Then clip again at a greater angle. Fusible interfacings prevent raveling so you can trim closer than normal.

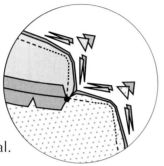

8. Press all seams flat as sewn, then press seams open over a matching shape on the June Tailor Board, if you have one.

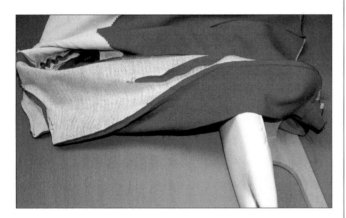

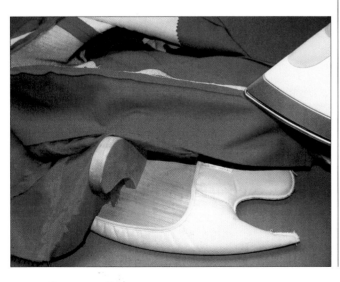

9. Turn the jacket to the right side and use a point turner to push out the corners of the collar and lapel. (Don't push your scissor points through your beautiful new collar, please!) We have found the bamboo point turner is sometimes rough, so we prefer the plastic one.

10. Roll seams to the under side. Press the edges and flatten with a wooden clapper.

NOTE: Pressing on a ham or the flat part of the June Tailor Board will lift the jacket off the table and help you press isolated edges without affecting other areas.

A ham worked great for pressing the neckline of this cardigan jacket.

Press from the underside in the collar and lapel area so you can make sure the seam barely rolls to the underside and it won't show.

The collar seam rolls to the underside.

From roll line down, press from the **facing side** so you can be sure the seam rolls to the underside. **Be sure to let your fabric cool thoroughly before moving.**

Join Collar Seams—Three Ways

Stitching the upper and under collar seams together controls them.

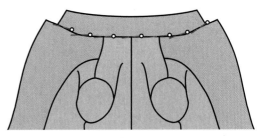

PRO Tip Depending on the thickness of your fabric and the amount of "turn-of-cloth" that the pattern has allowed, the neckline seams may not meet exactly. Do not adjust, but stitch them where they lie. If the upper collar curls up or the back neck seam shows, push the upper collar seam toward the back until the collar lies smoothly and covers the back neck seam. If you can't get it to cover the back neck seam, the collar is not wide enough. You can see this in tissue-fitting if you pin the collar to the jacket, but it is such a rare instance, we usually skip doing that!

Stab-stitch from the outside. With collar seams on top of each other, pin right through upper collar neck seam. On outside, stab-stitch collar sections together through wells of upper and under collar seams.

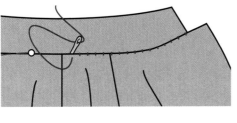

A stab stitch is a loose running stitch that joins two seams that fall on top of each other. The needle goes into the well of the seam on top at an angle and comes out of the well on under layer.

Catch-stitch from the inside. Fold neck facing out of the way and loosely catch the seams together.

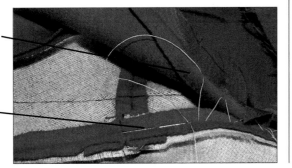

upper collar seam

under collar seam

Topstitch in the well of the seam. This is Marta's favorite way. Match seams and collars with pins on the upper collar.

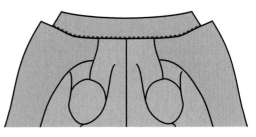

Now stitch in the ditch by machine.

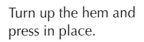

THE SEAM is finished! Pause, put your jacket on a coat hanger, hang it on the sewing room door and just sit back, admire your work and pat yourself on the back. It's a job well done.

Hem the Jacket

Trim the seam allowances in the hem area to 1/4" (6mm).

Turn up the hem and press in place.

PRO Tip

If the jacket hem is slightly flared, the hem edge will be larger than the jacket.

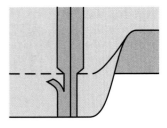

Steam the edge of the hem to shrink it. Be careful NOT to press over the edge or you could make an indent on the outside.

Now the hem fits the jacket without being wavy.

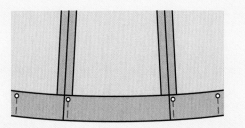

If steaming doesn't do the trick, run a 4-5mm machine basting stitch 1/4" from the edge and pull on the bobbin thread until the edge of the hem fits the jacket.

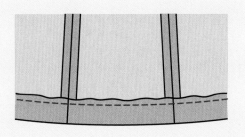

Hand sew **jacket** hem in place 1/4-1/2" below the edge, using a blind hem. This is a loose stitch done on inside of hem that makes a truly invisible hem. Use a size 10 sharp needle, catch only a fiber of your fabric, and make each stitch about 3/8" apart. **If you plan to machine sew the lining hem (Chapter 14), do not do this step now.**

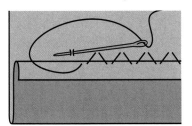

Hem the Jacket Lining

Hand sew the **lining** with a "jump" hem to allow movement and prevent the lining from ripping.

Or, you can machine hem the jacket and the lining together using the technique in Chapter 14.

1. Catch-stitch front facings to hem.

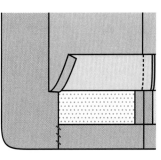

2. To allow lining to "move" so it won't pull out, turn under lower edge of lining 5/8" (1.5cm) and press. Match raw edges of the lining to jacket hem edge.

Slipstitch the lining to the jacket hem allowance along lining fold. When the thread is pulled tight, the stitches disappear.

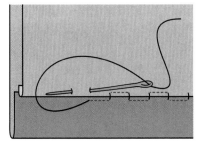

3. Smooth the extra length downward at front facing edges. Slipstitch front edges of lining to facing.

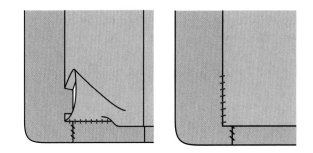

Hem the Sleeve Lining

Turn the sleeves wrong side out and smooth the lining sleeves so they are not twisted inside the armhole. Then turn under 5/8" on the lining and match the raw edge to the edge of the sleeve hem. Pin.

Sew the jacket sleeve hem by hand. Slipstitch in place. A "jump" hem will automatically form.

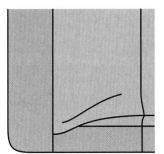

Steam-shape the Roll line

The last thing to do is to fold the collar and lapel on the roll lines. Place a towel under the front to protect the back. Steam just **above** the roll line to "set" the roll. Let it cool for 5 minutes before moving. With fusibles, you can re-shape a lapel any time. The resin on fusibles is "thermoplastic" and can be molded with heat. When cool, it "remembers" the new shape.

Sleeve Lining—Custom Method

Sue sews the sleeve lining into the jacket by hand. It eliminates the "floating" that can occur when the lining armholes are not firmly anchored.

1. Sew the lining to the facings, but don't set in the sleeves.

2. Sew the outside edges of the jacket and lining/facing unit and turn to the right side.

3. Hang the jacket on a hanger and pin the jacket and lining armholes together at the underarm.

4. Continue pinning the lining around armholes trimming away excess. (Remember, you have already trimmed the jacket sleeve underarm seam to 1/4".)

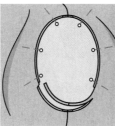

The lining shoulder seam may need to be deepened. If you could see through the already sewn-in jacket sleeve, it would look like this:

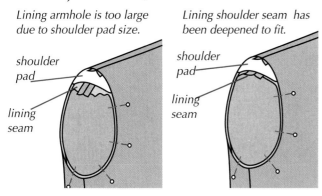

Lining armhole is too large due to shoulder pad size.

Lining shoulder seam has been deepened to fit.

shoulder pad

lining seam

shoulder pad

lining seam

NOTE: Deepen the lining shoulder seam only at armhole edge.

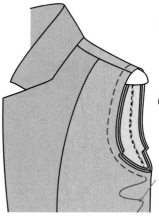

5. Hand baste armholes together, going through shoulder pads.

6. Sew lining sleeves.

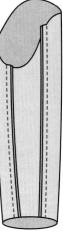

7. Ease the sleeve cap

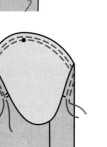

Quick Tip If your sleeve doesn't have a vent, first sew the lining and sleeve right sides together at the hem edge. Then hem the sleeve. Then pin the lining to the armhole.

8. Pin lining sleeves to armhole. Pull up on the ease threads as you turn under the seam allowance and pin.

9. Hand slip-stitch the sleeve lining securely in place to the jacket armhole seam using a double strand of thread. Do not catch the jacket in the stitching. The lining is now firmly anchored at the armhole.

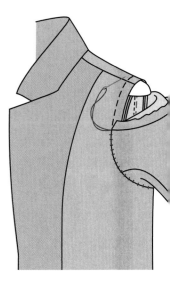

10. Sew the lining jump hem by hand unless you have already stitched by machine as in the Quick Tip above.

CHAPTER 14

Bagging a Lining

Bagging the lining is simply machine sewing the lining hem to the jacket and turning the jacket right side out through an opening in the sleeve. If the jacket has a back vent, it is easier to hand hem.

On page 93 in a Quick Tip, we suggested machine-basting for 8" in the middle of one sleeve seam or leave an 8" opening if you wanted to machine hem the jacket. In a 2-piece sleeve, the opening should be in the front seam as you will then avoid the eased area in the back seam when sewing the opening closed.

That "Tricky Little Front Bit"

No matter how many books on jackets and tailoring that we have looked through, we have not yet found one that tackles that final "tricky little bit" where the jump hem meets the front facing. Everyone resorts to sewing it by hand and for 35 years we have too! But the garment industry obviously doesn't. So, we have been on the search for that elusive "trick of the trade".

Lower edge of the lining is traditionally hand sewn to the facing and the facing to the hem.

This one is neatly and quickly machine finished using the "bagging" method.

Sue led us to two of Australia's finest fashion sewing teachers, Robin Nixon from Sydney and Rhonda Braybrook from Geelong. We extend them our thanks for sharing this very professional trick with you. Marta, in teaching tailoring workshops, refined the instructions and created the steps for our wonderful artist, Kate Pryka.

An Overview of Bagging

Your jacket is **right side out** and all edges are pressed. The collar seams are attached. The lining is not attached to the armholes or hem.

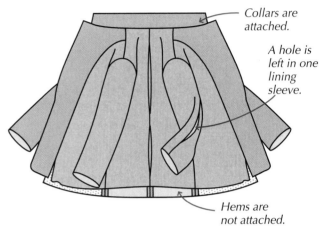

Collars are attached.

A hole is left in one lining sleeve.

Hems are not attached.

Now, turn the jacket wrong sides out through the opening at the hem. Stitch the hem edges together. Then turn the jacket right side out through the hole in the sleeve.

The Important Reminders

THE HEM DOT is VERY important in making the "bagging" technique EASY and ACCURATE!

Place the **facing** pattern over the **front** pattern to mark THE HEM DOT.

On the **facing** pattern, THE HEM DOT is 5/8" from lower edge and 5/8" in from edge where lining is attached.

On the jacket **front** pattern, THE HEM DOT is where the hemline intersects the facing seams.

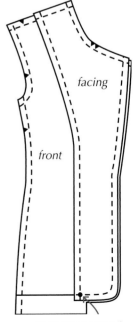

facing

front

THE HEM DOT for that "tricky little bit"

Quick Tip Use a pen that will penetrate through both tissues at the same time when marking THE HEM DOT.

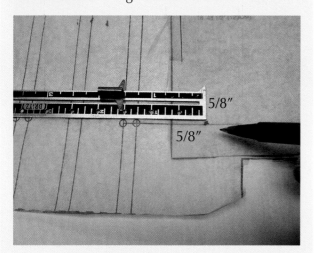

Transfer THE HEM DOT marking from the tissue to the jacket and the facing.

Your Jacket is Ready to Machine Hem

You have sewn the outside seam of the jacket to THE HEM DOTS on both sides of the lower fronts and backstitched carefully. (See page 95.)

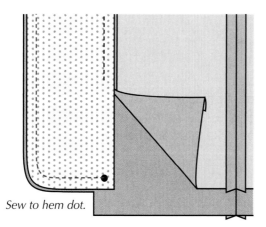

Sew to hem dot.

You have trimmed the outside seam, pressed it open, turned the jacket facing to the right side and pressed the front edge. Now you are ready for the bagging technique.

You have pressed up the hem to establish the hem crease.

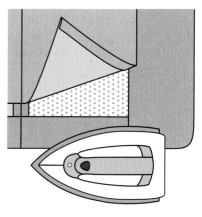

You have trimmed the seam allowances in the hem area to 1/4" to reduce bulk.

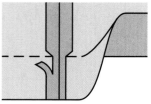

Turn the jacket inside out to begin the "bagging" process.

Bag the Lining

1. Match lower edges of lining and jacket, right sides together. Pin.

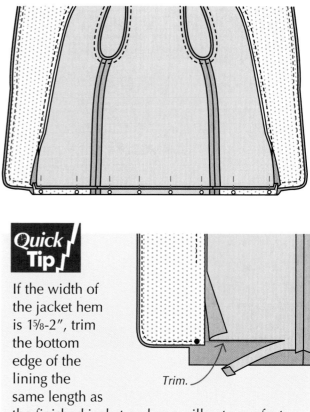

Quick Tip If the width of the jacket hem is 1⅝-2", trim the bottom edge of the lining the same length as the finished jacket and you will get a perfect "jump hem" (see page 99).

Trim.

2. Sew edges together with a 3/8" seam allowance.

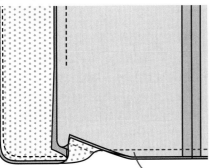

Sew lining to jacket hem edge here.

Quick Tip If the lining and jacket hem edges aren't exactly a perfect fit, usually you can stretch one or the other to make them fit, which is essentially easing one to the other. Otherwise, you need to resew the vertical lining seams where necessary until the hem edges fit and seams match.

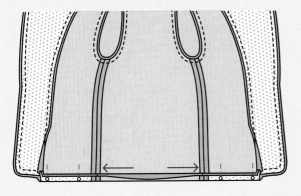

3. This is the beginning of that "tricky little front bit." Clip ONLY the JACKET FRONT to the hemline dot.

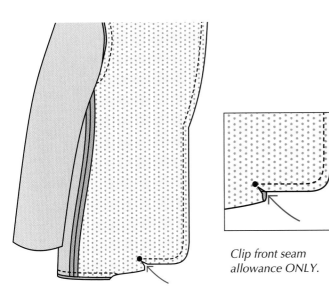

Clip front seam allowance ONLY.

4. Fold jacket hem right sides together along hemline crease. Smooth lining down the edge of the facing. The lining will have a fold at the bottom.

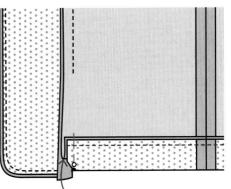

lining fold

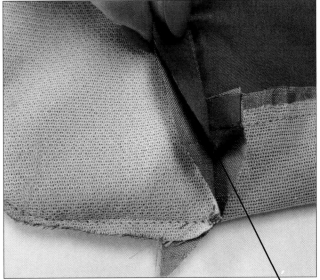

This is the fold you will see between the facing and the hem.

5. Fold the facing out of the way. Finish stitching the lining to the facing through THE HEM DOT to the lower edge. Backstitch. The seam will look like this from the lining side.

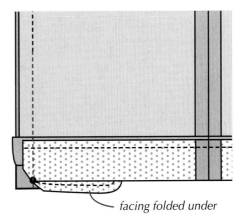

facing folded under

103

It will look like this from the jacket side.

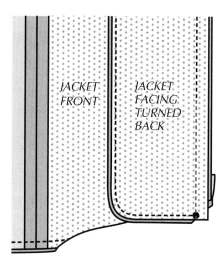

JACKET FRONT

JACKET FACING TURNED BACK

6. Slash the corners to eliminate some of the bulk.

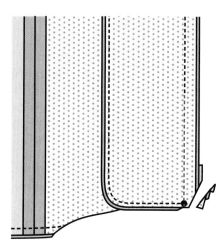

The seam allowances on the facing edge will go toward the lining.

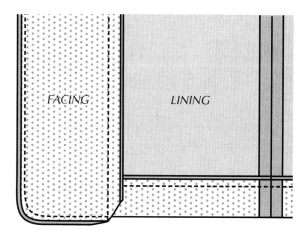

FACING

LINING

7. Turn the jacket through the hole in the sleeve. (Make sure you have removed ALL pins before turning as it will be hard to get inside the jacket later.) You will be AMAZED at how nice the lining looks at the hem and facing edge! Carefully give it a final press.

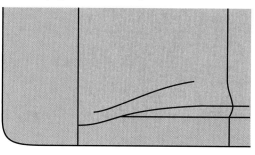

The jacket lining now has a "jump" hem. To secure the hem, stitch in the well of the seams by hand or by machine. Sew from the RIGHT side of the jacket to make sure the stitches are invisible.

Stitch in the well of the seam for 1½".

If a jacket has only side seams, you will also need to catch the hem in a few more places. Hand stitch through the hem invisibly to the right side. Or, for a sporty look machine top-stitch the hem instead.

Finish the Sleeve Hem

Non-vented sleeves—Turn up hem and press.

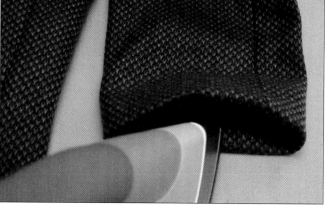

Put your arms into the sleeves to straighten the lining, making sure the lining sleeves aren't twisted. Pin one pin at the underarm seam through lining and fashion fabric to keep the lining and sleeve from twisting when the jacket is turned.

Reach through opening in the lining sleeve and pull the jacket and lining sleeves out. Remove the first pin and with the hem edges wrong sides

together, pin, matching seams. (Again, make sure you have not twisted the lining sleeve.)

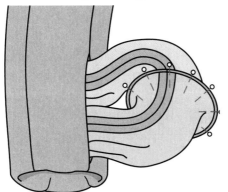

Sew the hem edges right sides together using a 3/8" seam allowance.

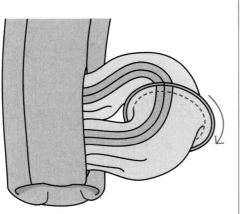

"Do as we say, not as we do!"

You can hand-hem sleeves now or use the hemming QUICK TIP below.

Put the sleeves back through the sleeve lining opening. Check again to make sure lining sleeve isn't twisted.

 If you didn't hand hem, pin up hem and stitch in the well of the seams to anchor the hems. If you have a 2-piece sleeve, this will hold the hems up! Hand hem 1-piece sleeves.

Vented sleeves—Hand hem as on page 99.

Close the Sleeve Opening

Close the opening in the lining sleeve with a hand slipstitch.

Stitch the opening closed with a machine edgestitch, as is done in ready-mades.

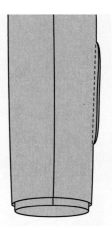

NOTE: The first time Pati tried the bagging technique, she sewed the lining to the sleeve hem before the jacket was turned right side out, hoping to be able to COMPLETELY finish ALL of the edges by machine! OOPS!

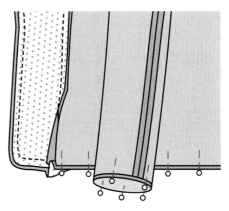

CHAPTER 15

Buttonholes

Machine Buttonholes

Types

Standard sewing machine buttonholes are great in casual jackets. Machine stitched keyhole buttonholes are generally used in blazers and menswear and are very much the look of the moment. Many mid-to-top-of-the-line sewing machines offer an excellent selection. Bound buttonholes are traditional in

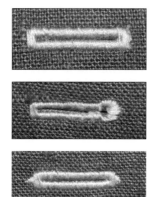

Buttonholes courtesy of Husqvarna/Viking

dressy suits and coats, and they come and go with fashion. They also become the buttonhole of choice when thread matching is an issue.

Tips for Good Quality Machine Buttonholes

◆ Always test buttonholes on the same fabric, with the same interfacing as the garment and with a seam like the front edge of a jacket.

◆ Make sure both sides of the buttonhole rows look the same. If not, check your machine manual for adjustment possibilities.

◆ Try stitching with a larger needle and buttonhole twist on the top spool. If you can't get the perfect color in buttonhole twist, or if your machine can't handle it, try two spools of regular thread on the top, threaded simultaneously. Or, if you have perfect control, stitch over the same buttonhole twice with a single thread.

◆ Try cording your buttonhole to give it more depth and richness.

◆ Some machines sew a "handmade-look" keyhole buttonhole. OR, find a tailor to hand-sewn

keyhole buttonholes for you. They may cost $5 to $6 each, a beautiful touch and worth every penny! Always take your own thread, because tailors usually sew only men's classic colors. Also, always thread-mark the position and length so the tailor remembers that you want your jacket to wrap right over left, the opposite of men's jackets. Look in the phone book for tailors in your area.

Tips for Sewing on Buttons

The number, style and type of buttons are a personal choice. Remember the following button "rules:"

◆ If there are buttons near the waist and bust, to prevent gaping, position buttons in those locations for YOUR body.

◆ Unless you have a vent in the hem, don't put a button below the waist level. You won't be able to sit without undoing it or wrinkling the front.

◆ All buttons need a shank. For sew-through buttons, place a toothpick on top of button and sew to garment over the toothpick. Remove the toothpick and wrap thread around the loose threads between the button and the garment. After a few wraps, secure the thread.

NOTE: Even shank buttons are more stable when you wrap the threads.

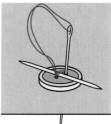

Shank and sew-through style buttons.

An easy way to create a shank is to fold the fabric back at the location at which you want to sew on the button. Place the button under the fold with the holes the same distance from the fold as the length of the shank you want.

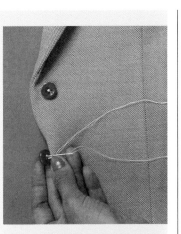

After stitching through the button and fold several times, wrap the thread around the first stitches, forming a shank. Knot the thread in the fold.

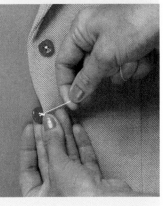

◆ If you have loosely woven fabric or think there will be stress on the buttons, sew a reinforcing button on the under side, directly under each fashion button. A reinforcing button is usually a small, flat clear plastic button that is stitched simultaneously with the fashion button. (The fashion button still needs a shank.) This is done on Ultrasuede.

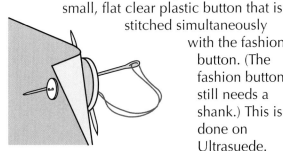

◆ Non-functional sew-through buttons, like those on a sleeve vent, should be sewn without a shank and can even be sewn on by machine. Use a button foot or remove the foot and lower the presser bar. Check your machine's manual.

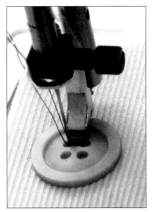

◆ To make thread stronger for sewing on buttons, run it through beeswax or Thread Heaven. To make it smooth, press the thread with an iron.

◆ An easy way to cut open a machine buttonhole is to use the buttonhole cutter. Before cutting, run your fingernail back and forth between the rows of the buttonhole to separate the stitching. Center the cutter between the rows of stitching and press down firmly.

Prevent Stretch in Buttonholes

STABILIZE

"Tear-away" stabilizer or a patch of no-stretch interfacing under the buttonhole will help control stretch.

CORD

Stitch buttonholes over cording or heavy-weight thread to strengthen buttonholes and enhance the look of the satin stitching. Check your machine's manual for tips. Stitch over but not through the cord. When buttonhole is completed, pull on cording ends until the loop disappears. With a hand sewing needle, bring loose cord ends to the wrong side. Tie and clip.

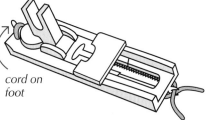

cord on foot

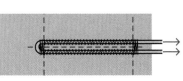

Bound Buttonholes

Bound buttonholes are beautiful and durable and not hard to make once you develop a "system." They are easiest to do before the jacket front is attached to the other pieces. All horizontal buttonholes begin 1/8" (3mm) from center front toward the edge. Plan the length according to the diameter and thickness of the button. It is a good idea to make a TEST buttonhole first to check the fashion fabric performance and buttonhole size. (This is particularly important if your button has excess depth or is an unusual shape. Slip button through to make sure it fits!)

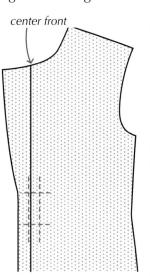

center front

Mark Carefully!

Mark the center front and ends of buttonhole on the interfacing side of the right front. (See page 62 for marking tips.) Machine baste on these lines through interfacing and fashion fabric to transfer markings to right side. Change the bobbin to a contrasting color thread for easy-to-see markings.

Here are three of our favorite methods:

Organza Patch Method

1. Pin bias strips of silk organza 1" (2.5cm) longer than buttonhole and 1½" (3.75cm) wide on the **RIGHT** side of the garment, centered over placement lines. The color of organza doesn't need to match your fabric as it disappears in the finished buttonhole.

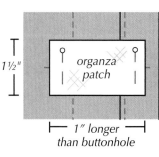

1½"

organza patch

⊢— 1" longer —⊣
than buttonhole

NOTE: Ambiance rayon or Sun Silky lining can be used, as can cotton organdy, if silk organza can't be found.

2. Machine baste through the center of the organza. (This is easiest to do from wrong side following the basting lines.)

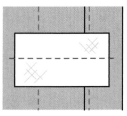

3. Using small stitches, sew a rectangle the length of the buttonhole and 1/4 - 1/8"-wide (3mm-6mm) on each side of the center line. Lightly draw these lines on the organza with

a pencil or use your presser foot as a guide. Start and stop stitching at the "X", overlapping stitches, to avoid weak corners. Check all rectangles—they must be on grain and the same size, with square corners. Remove basting.

4. Clip rectangle to corners, right next to a stitch.

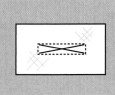

NOTE: If buttonhole is long, cut through the center and then form wedges at each end.

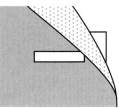

5. Turn organza to wrong side to form "window." Press.

PRO Tip First anchor the organza by pinning into a ham.

6. Cut a piece of fusible web with a rectangle cut out of the center the size of buttonhole window.

Quick Tip Fold a rectangle of web in half and clip out a piece half the length of the buttonhole opening and 1/4" (6mm) wide.

7. Place the web on the wrong side of buttonhole over the lining patch. "Steam-baste" the web in place by lightly steaming above it until it becomes tacky and adheres to the organza patch. (Do not touch iron to the web!)

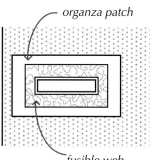

organza patch

fusible web

 Steam-A-Seam ® is a tacky fusible web that will stay in place without steaming. Stick 1/4" strips around the opening. Remove paper.

8. Cut two rectangles of fashion fabric 1½" wide (3.75cm) and 1" (2.5cm) longer than buttonholes. Lips should be on the straight of grain unless the fabric is a plaid; then use bias. Baste through the center of the two rectangles, right sides together. Press open to form the lips.

9. Center the lips under the window and steam-baste them in place from the top side by slightly melting the fusible web. Don't press down heavily to avoid imprints from the welts through to the right side. Use a press cloth if necessary. Lips will now stay in place without slipping during stitching.

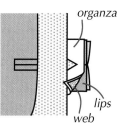

organza

lips

web

10. Fold back fashion fabric, exposing long sides. Stitch long sides, then ends.

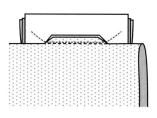

11. Trim and grade back side of buttonhole.

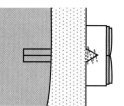

 Sew the same end of all the buttonholes at one time.

 Using the Organza Patch method, you can make buttonholes (or pockets) ANY shape. Try triangles, circles, squares, or abstract shapes—let your imagination run wild!

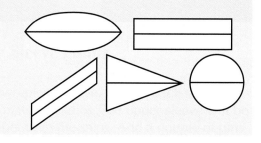

Strip Method Corded Bound Buttonhole

Cording keeps the lips from "sinking" into the jacket front. It improves the look of these bound buttonholes in all but heavy wool coatings.

NOTE: Always make a sample first as explained on page 109.

1. Mark placement lines on right front. See page 62 for marking tips.

2. Cut a strip of fabric the length of the buttonhole plus 1" (2.5cm), and about 1 ½" (3.75cm) wide. Strip may be straight grain or bias.

 Cut one long strip for all buttonholes. Snip apart as needed.

3. Fold the strip in half, wrong sides together. Place a narrow string or cording (preshrunk) in the fold.

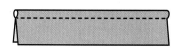

4. Adjust the zipper foot so the needle hits just next to the cord. Or, use a piping/cording foot.

cording foot

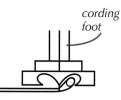

5. To aid stitching and reduce bulk, trim one raw edge to the exact width of the stitched cord.

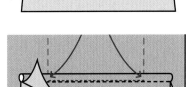

6. Center strip over vertical basting lines on the garment side, with short raw edge against horizontal basting line. Stitch, on top of original stitching using a short stitch length. Start and stop at the vertical markings. Backstitch at each end.

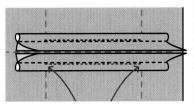

7. Place raw edge of second strip against the first strip's raw edge. The untrimmed edges now form a "tent." Stitch on top of the original stitching between the vertical markings.

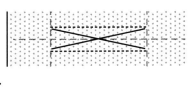

8. From the wrong side, clip an X through all layers except the buttonhole strips.

9. Turn strips to inside and tug lightly on the strips to straighten the lips and corners. Fold back the fashion fabric exposing the ends.

10. Stitch the triangle ends as shown.

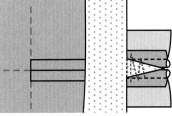

Sue's Favorite Bound Buttonhole Method

Sue uses the double-welt pocket method without the pocket bag for her buttonholes! See page 69.

Marta's Method for Finishing the Back of a Bound Buttonhole

After the facing is attached and pressed in place, slit the facing exactly in the center of the buttonhole. Turn the edge under and slip stitch.

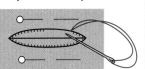

Triangular Bound Buttonholes

A triangular buttonhole can be used as a buttonhole or welt pocket. These can be on the horizontal or at a slant.

This technique originally appeared in our book *Couture, The Art of Fine Sewing* by Roberta Carr. The book has tons of creative ideas and tips that will enhance your skills.

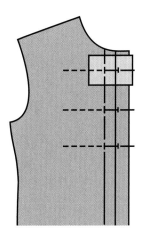

1. Determine buttonhole placement and chalk-mark the placement lines on the wrong side of the garment. Hand baste on these lines to transfer markings to the right side.

2. Cut a 4" X 6" (10 X 15 cm) rectangle from fashion fabric or contrast fabric for a 1"-1½" (2.5-3.75cm) buttonhole. Cut so the cross grain goes through the center of the buttonhole.

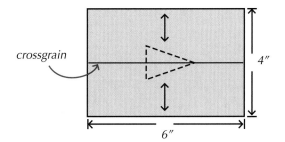

3. Pin patch to garment front, right sides together. Chalk center front of garment and the width of the buttonhole.

4. Draw a triangle on the patch with sharp chalk and a ruler. Be precise. Allow the lines to cross at each point for absolute accuracy.

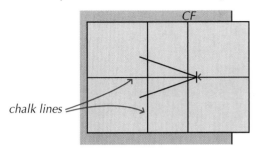

chalk lines

CF

4. Begin and end at the middle of one long side, overlapping stitches. Sew with a stitch length of 1.5mm. Take two small stitches across the corners rather than pivoting.

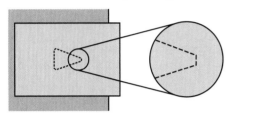

5. To create the hole through which to turn the button-hole, cut through the center of the triangle and into each corner, though all layers. Be sure to cut accurately down the center of the triangle as these will become the two lips.

Cut through all layers.

6. Make three slashes through the patch only, cutting from the outer edge of the patch to within 1/8″ of the corners of the stitched triangle.

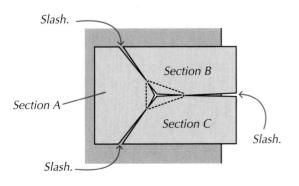

Slash.

Section A

Section B

Section C

Slash.

Slash.

7. Pull section A through cut in triangle to wrong side. Press firmly so it does not show on the right side. Flatten with the clapper.

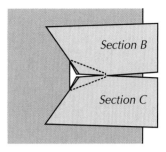

Section B

Section C

NOTE: It is easier if you work on top of a ham.

8. From the right side, fold sections B and C toward the center of the buttonhole and press firmly against the seams.

9. Then pull these sections those through to inside. Wrap patch fabric around the two lip edges in the center of the buttonhole to create lips. Press from wrong side. Check right side to be sure lips are even and pucker-free.

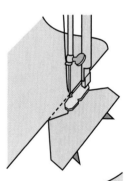

10. On the inside, turn the garment back to expose the small triangular tab under section A. Use a zipper foot to sew tab to patch. Stitch through all layers.

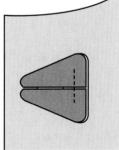

11. Trim away excess fabric on patch, rounding corners.

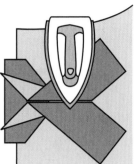

Triangular buttonholes in plaids look great when the lips are on the bias.

CHAPTER 16

More Pockets

In-seam Pockets

The easiest pockets are in-seam pockets and they do not add any bulk. They will look best if there is a fabric extension to which the pocket pieces are sewn.

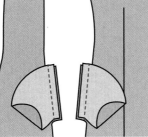

1. Sew the pocket bags to the front and side front or to front and back.

2. Press seams toward pocket.

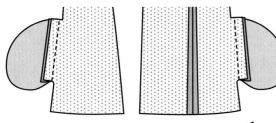

3. Sew the side seams, basting across the pocket opening. Be sure to backstitch at the top and bottom of the opening.

4. Stitch around the pocket.

Clip back to stitching.

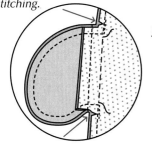

5. Clip the back seam allowance close to the stitching. Press the pocket toward the front; press remaining seams open.

Single-Welt Pockets

Single-welt pockets are often slanted when on the upper left of a jacket. Lower welt pockets are generally straight. On a loose coat they can be vertical.

1. Cut the welt according to the pattern.

2. Fuse interfacing to the wrong side of the welt. Sew the short ends right sides together. Trim and clip the corners. Turn and press. If you want to topstitch, do it now.

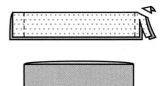

3. For lower pocket welts, cut two 8″ X 8″ squares per pocket from lining. For upper pocket welts, cut two 6″ X 6″ lining squares.

4. Machine baste on right side exactly where welt will be sewn.

5. On the wrong side, center a 3″ X 8″ rectangle of regular Pellon over the basting line to stabilize the welt. Pin.

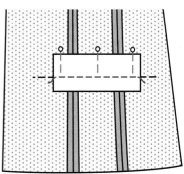

6. Place welt on right side so the raw edge laps 1/4″ over welt basting. Stitch on welt, beginning and ending exactly at the ends of the welt. Back stitch very carefully so no stitches fall beyond welt.

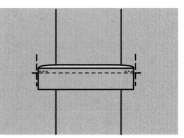

7. On right side, place one square of the lining fabric over the welt, matching the top edges. On the wrong side, stitch exactly on the first stitching line.

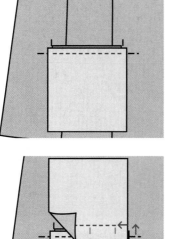

8. On right side, pin second lining square so it overlaps previous stitching by 1/4" (6mm).

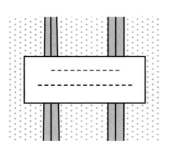

9. On wrong side, stitch 1/2" (1.3mm) above the first row of stitching. This stitching is 1/2" shorter than the lower row at each end.

10. On the wrong side, cut though the center of the two rows of stitches through garment and Pellon only, not through the lining. Cut diagonally to the corner. The angle will look odd.

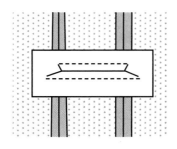

11. Turn lining to right side and pull pocket pieces through opening. Press the welt carefully using your ham to support it.
The pocket ends will not match.

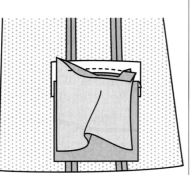

12. Stitch around the pocket, curving the bottom corners to prevent lint from collecting in them.

Catch the pie-shaped wedges while stitching.

13. On the right side, carefully stitch the ends of the welt to the jacket front. This can be done by hand or top-stitched by machine. This stitching will catch the pie-shaped wedges.

Inside Pockets

An inside pocket is generally about 1" into the facing and about 4" long. It is sewn just like any double-welt pocket (page 69). You can use jacket or lining fabric for the welts. In the jacket below, the piping and welts are from a man's tie. **For a ladies' jacket, the pocket is placed BELOW the bust area.**

Marta added narrow self-fabric ties to the sides of the patch pockets as she lined them. After the pockets were slip stitched to the jacket, she tied them together.

Creative Pocket Ideas

There are many possible pocket variations. Here are some ideas. Patch pocket instructions are on page 66, welt pockets on page 69.

wider at the top to make a pleat

embroidered pockets

Pocket goes to hem.

bias patch pockets with flaps

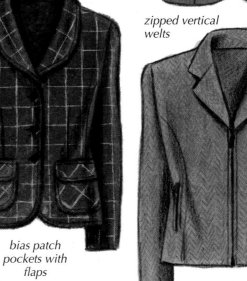

zipped vertical welts

Use a zipper in place of welts. Make a window as for bound buttonhole on page 110. Place a zipper under the opening and edgestitch around the window to hold the zipper in place. Add pocket bags.

Flaps come in many shapes.

CHAPTER 17
Easy Mitered Back Vent

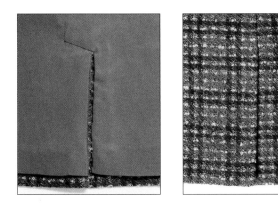

Vents are in and out of fashion, but they are a sharp-looking feature on a jacket. Also, since the vent can open when you sit, it lessens wrinkling in the front of your jacket. Mitering is a super clean finish for the bottom of the left vent. It is easy to do too!

1. Sew the center back seam to the circle at the top of the vent.

2. Snip the **right** back seam allowance to the center of the last stitch at the circle.

   NOTE: When we say right and left back, we mean when the jacket is on your body.

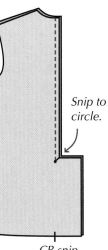

Snip to circle.

CB snip

3. Press the vent extension towards the left back from the bottom of the center back seamline to the center back snip at the bottom.

4. Press under the 5/8" (1.5cm) seam allowance on the right vent.

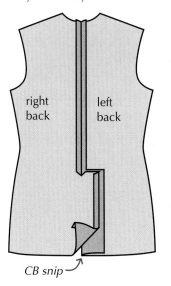

right back   left back

CB snip

5. At the top of the vent, grade the edges by trimming 1/4" (6mm) off the right vent. Catch-stitch both top edges in place to underlining or with a fine needle to fashion fabric.

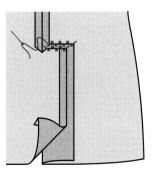

NOTE: Make certain your jacket is the right length. It can't be changed after mitering. Also, the miter looks best if the hem and vent depths are the same.

6. Fold up the hem allowance and snip the intersection where the edges meet.

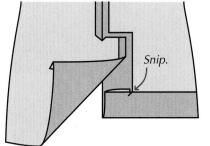

Snip.

7. Unfold and line up the snips.

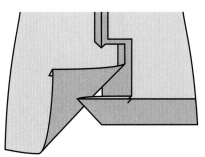

8. Trim from the snip to the corner leaving ¼ seam allowances.

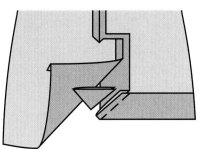

NOTE: Marta skips this step and folds right sides together from snips to corner. Pati prefers to first pin along the seamline and trim for more accuracy. Try both ways.

9. Turn right sides together and stitch a 1/4" seam.

10. Diagonally trim the seam at the corner to eliminate bulk. Turn and press.

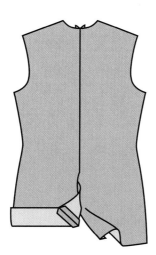

11. Right sides together, fold up the hem allowance on the right back vent. Stitch the edges of the under vent together on the 5/8" seam line. Trim, turn and press.

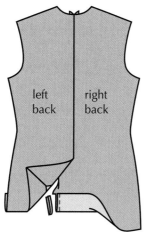

NOTE: Left and right refers to when the jacket is on your body. A vent is like a lapped zipper from the right side, it laps left over right.

The Goof-Proof Back Vent in a Lining

Have you ever had problems figuring out which side of the lining in the vent area is to be cut away? This one is goof-proof!

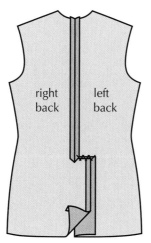

NOTE: This same method can be used on the left back vent of a skirt.

1. Cut out the lining.

2. Mark the cutaway section with tracing paper on both back pieces. Do not cut anything out of vent area yet.

3. Sew center back seam to large dot.

4. Lay lining on jacket wrong sides together. Cut away **left** back.

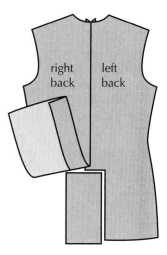

Left and right back refer to the lining when on the body.

5. Staystitch corner on left back. Clip to stitching.

6. On LEFT back lining, press under 5/8" (1.5cm) above and below clipped corner. On RIGHT back lining, press under 3/4" on long edge of extension.

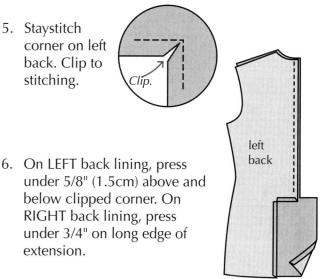

Finishing the Back Vent

After hemming the lining, slipstitch the lining to the vent.

Save work—machine stitch the right vent and lining edges together. Calvin Klein does!

Hand slip-stitch top and long edge of left vent.

For long vents like those on coats, topstitch top edges of vent together through all layers.

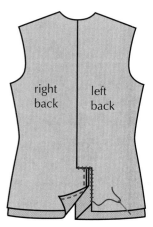

CHAPTER 18
Finishing Touches

Topstitching and Edgestitching

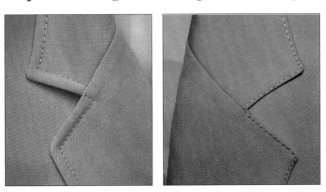

Topstitching is 1/4" (6mm) from the edge. Edgestitching is as close to the edge as you can sew.

The Notch

Topstitch the collar. Pivot at the gorge line and stitch in the well of the seam to the notch. Pivot and stitch for 1/4". Pivot and continue topstitching the lapel.

Four Ways to Stitch Straight and Evenly

throat plate guide   *presser foot with needle 1/4" from edge*

1/4" quilting foot   *quilting guide for wide topstitching.*

Thread

Silk or polyester buttonhole twist, or two strands of regular sewing thread, shows up well, and is generally used in the needle only.

A blazer lapel folds to the outside, so when using topstitching thread, stitch on the upper collar and facing and stop at the bottom of the roll line. Flip jacket over and continue stitching on jacket right side.

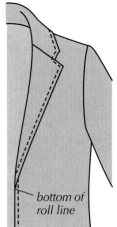

bottom of roll line

Tie and bury threads.

Pull all threads to the wrong side.

Thread all ends through a large-eye needle. Tie a knot or backstitch to secure. Stick the needle into the seamline and come out 1" away.

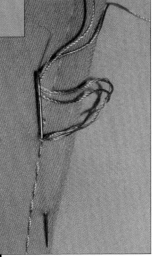

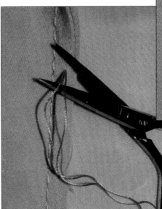

Cut off the threads close to the fabric. A slight tug will pull the threads below the surface.

Needles

The thicker the thread, the larger the needle must be. Use 16-18 (European 100-110) size needles. To solve skipped stitch problems, try a topstitching needle and stitch slowly.

Stitch Length

A longer stitch (4 or 5mm) shows up better. Short stitches bury themselves in heavier fabrics.

Make Your Own Bias Strips

Bias is used for binding a seam or edge and for piping. Possible fabric ideas are men's ties, silk, and lining fabric in prints or solids. If you use Ultrasuede or Ultraleather, use the crosswise grain, which has more give than the lengthwise grain and will bend around corners like bias.

To get TRUE bias, fold the crosswise grain so it is parallel to the length-wise grain. The fold is the perfect bias.

To cut even bias strips, use a rotary cutter and mat with a ruler.

When piecing bias, place the strips at right angles to each other and sew on the straight grain rather than across the bias. Stitching begins where the two strips come together.

Press the seam open.
The seam won't stretch because it is on the straight grain.

Making Piping

To make piping, fold a 1½"-wide strip (3.75 cm) over preshrunk cotton cording or the softer rattail rayon and sew next to the cording with a zipper foot or cording foot.

Insert Piping

Sew piping to your jacket with piping stitching line exactly on garment stitching line. Use your "piping" foot if you have one.

Use double-stick basting tape to hold it while sewing.

Place jacket facing on top, making a piping sandwich. (Sewing from garment side on top of the first row of stitching is easiest.)

Adding piping to the outside edge of a shawl collar is easy. It also looks expensive, especially using a synthetic suede or leather as the piping.

For more on sewing synthetic suedes and leathers, see *Sewing Ultrasuede Fabrics*.

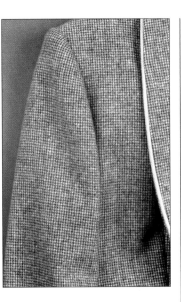

Piped Lining

Add a piping to the edge of a facing before attaching the lining. Below we have used a man's tie for a coordinating piping and the matching welts of and inside pocket.

 Be sure to tuck under the raw edges at the end of the piping when attaching it to the facing.

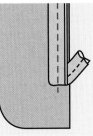

Decorative Seam and Edge Finishes

Heavy rayon thread was used in the upper looper of a serger to flatlock the lining and facing together on this plaid jacket. See our serger books and videos for how-tos.

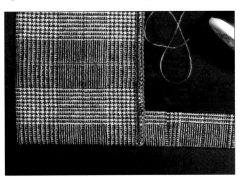

Variegated cotton crochet thread was used in the upper looper of a serger to finish the facing, hem, and seam edges of this unlined wool knit jacket.

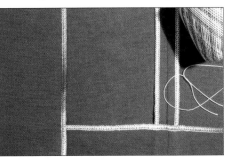

Pocket Lining Doubles as Hanky

The "hanky" is really the pocket bag of this single-welt pocket.

CHAPTER 19

TIPS That Will Improve ALL of Your Sewing

Because we teach hands-on sewing workshops, we learn a lot about sewing skills. When we train beginning sewing teachers at our workshops in Portland, Oregon, we ask them to pretend to become beginners again and take the same course they will be teaching. They are amazed at some of the things they missed when they learned to sew. Many sewers today are self-taught. This chapter is a TIP chapter and will include the "mini lessons" we often teach in our workshops. Above all, know your machine WELL so it works FOR you!

 PERFECT PRINCESS SEAMS

◆ The cut edges will NOT match, but the seamlines will. Therefore, when cutting, be sure to snip the markings above and below the most curved area so you can match the edges properly.

◆ Staystitch 1/2" from the edge between snips on the inside (concave) curve on the FRONT.

◆ Pin the front to the side front, clipping seam allowances on the inside (concave) curve as necessary to fit the outside (convex) curve. The greater the curve, the more you will need to clip.

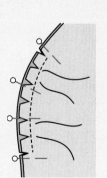

◆ Always sew with the inside curve on top.

 SEW WITH WHICH SIDE ON TOP?

◆ Sew with stable side on top. This includes the side with a lining, stay tape, interfacing, or staystitching.

◆ Sew with the side to be eased on the bottom next to the feed dogs on your machine. They will help you do the easing.

EXCEPTION:

◆ When setting in a sleeve, it is easier to be accurate with the sleeve on top.

UNDERSTITCHING

After sewing the facing to the front of this cardigan jacket, we understitched on only one side to show you the difference it made. To understitch, sew through all seam allowances from the facing side next to the seamline.

Usually, pressing the seam open first, then pressing it toward the facing side is enough to have a sharp edge and the seam rolled to the under side. Collarless "V" necklines are often an exception.

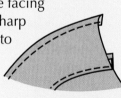

With no understitching, the facing shows.

With understitching, the facing stays under.

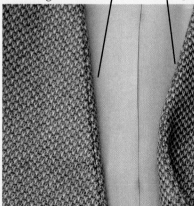
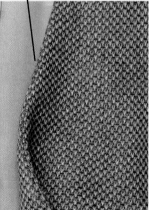

PATIENCE AND MEMORY SAVERS

- A shot-of-steam iron saves time and improves the quality of your finished garment.
- TWO seam rolls enable you to press another seam while one cools.

- Snipping notches helps your memory.
- Fuse interfacings then pin pieces so they are ready to fit. Pin lining seams so they are ready to sew. Psychologically you will feel ahead.
- Sew as many jacket and lining seams as possible at one time; then press all at one time.

 **STAYSTITCHING**

Staystitching is a row of regular stitches in the seam allowance next to the seamline and is used to stabilize bias. Today, we don't handle the fabric as much as we did in custom tailoring. Also, fusible interfacings help keep the fabric stable. But we do still staystitch the neckline before attaching the collar. For more details on "directional staystitching," see our book *Mother Pletsch's Painless Sewing*.

 YOU END UP WITH TWO LEFT SLEEVES

Or you end up with two right fronts. Why? You separated the pieces without marking them or pinning them to a corresponding piece. SOLUTION: Mark the wrong side of fronts with chalk and, before fusing, make sure you have a mirror image.

For two-piece sleeves, pin right sides together immediately after separating the pieces.

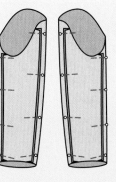

KEEP MACHINE NEEDLES ORGANIZED

Marta has two ways to keep her sewing machine needles organized. She color-codes new needles. She runs a colored permanent marker across them while they're in the box.

When she changes needles, she puts them in a pin cushion according to size.

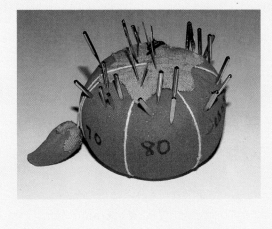

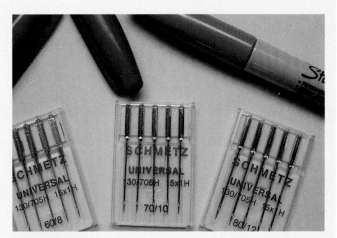

KEEP PATTERN HANDY

Keep your pattern pieces out after cutting and until the jacket is done. Why? You will often need a quick reference for markings or to see if something has shrunk, grown, or stretched.

CHAPTER 20
Plaids and Stripes

It seems either stripes or plaids are always somewhere on the fashion scene, so no book on sewing jackets can ignore them. Our space is short, so we are giving you the most important considerations.

Yardage

Always buy extra yardage to allow for matching plaids. Usually 1/4-1/2 yard extra is sufficient, depending on the size of the repeat of the plaid.

Even plaids are easier to work with than uneven.

*Even plaid—
When folded on the bias,the edges match in all directions.*

*Uneven plaid—
When folded on the bias, the edges will not match in one or both directions.*

An uneven plaid requires extra planning. If its horizontal bars are uneven, then you must use a directional pattern layout, as for napped fabrics. If the vertical bars are uneven, then the repeats do not have a center from which to balance the design in both directions from the jacket center front or back. Such a plaid will have to go around the body in one direction-unless the fabric is reversible. Then you can reverse the pattern pieces on one side of the garment so the jacket left and right mirror each other. Either way, place the same dominant bar at center front and back.

Layout and Matching Tips

- Match stitching lines, not cutting lines.
- Match the front armhole notch on the sleeve and the front of garment.
- Match side seams, center back and front horizontally.
- Place prominent bars in the center of the garment or balanced on each side of the center.
- Watch the prominent **horizontal** bar placement. Do you want it at the widest part of your bust or hip?
- Match pockets to where they will be attached to the jacket or cut them on the bias.
- If you are making a plaid skirt to go with the jacket, make sure the center fronts and backs match vertically.
- Bars will **not match** at these locations: raglan seams, shoulder seams, darts, above bust darts at sides, princess seams above the bust, back armhole and sleeve, or in any gathered or eased area.
- Before cutting, use a square ruler to make sure plaids are square. Match **BOTH** edges of the ruler to the plaid lines, not just one as in this photo.

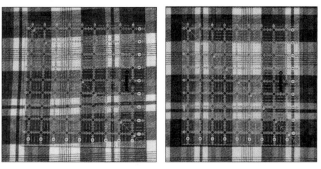

Plaids match sides of ruler, but not top and bottom.

Plaids match all 4 sides of square ruler.

Match the front sleeve notch to the front armhole notch. Center the sleeve on a plaid line.

Place the facing on the front and draw some of the plaid lines on the tissue to match the front.

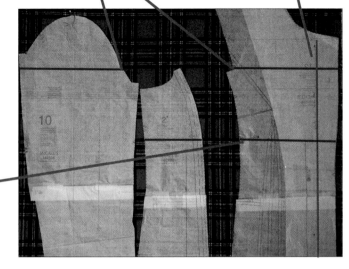

Match the notches just below the bust curve and the side seams will match to the hem.

Sewing Stripes and Plaids

You can use double-stick basting tape to get a perfect match.

Place tape next to the stitching line on one layer. Peel off protective paper. Press the seam allowance under on the other layer. Stick fold to tape.

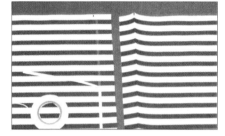

We have lapped the collar dot and neckline seam of the collar to the jacket and drawn some matching lines on the collar.

The pocket tissue was placed on the front and matching lines drawn on it for placement on the fabric.

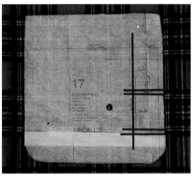

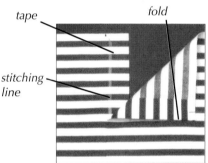

tape

fold

stitching line

Cutting Tips

Stop spending hours trying to match two layers of plaids perfectly before cutting.

Cut the top layer, remove excess fabric around it. Remove pattern. If top layer doesn't match under layer, move it until it matches exactly.

Then cut under layer which matches so well, you can't see it!

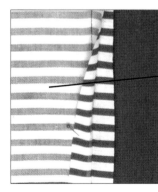

Flip the right side over to the left and stitch in the crease.

Remove the tape and press seam. VOILA! Perfectly matched stripes or plaids.

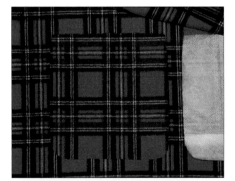

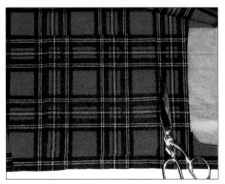

CHAPTER 21
Men's Jackets

Photo courtesy of Vogue Pattern Co.

Our best advice is that men's tailoring is very much the same as tailoring a woman's blazer jacket with pockets. Sometimes it's just larger pattern pieces. Many men, however, do need a high round back alteration to keep their jacket from hiking up in the back. See page 35.

Men's jackets are different from women's in the following construction techniques:

◆ Extra layers of interfacing are placed in the front chest and shoulder area. These can include polyester fleece.

◆ Buttonholes are made in the left front.

◆ Hand or machine keyhole buttonholes are used.

◆ The jacket back is softer, rarely underlined, and often just partially lined.

◆ There is usually an inside pocket in the upper chest over the lining/facing seam.

Fabrics - Wool tweed is the best choice for a first menswear project as it is always fashion-right, simple to sew, and often reasonable in price. (See No Fail Fabrics, page 15-20 for other choices.)

Front interfacing - Fuse according to manufacturer's instructions. We use interfacing the same way we do in women's jackets.

Chest Piece -
Cut extra layers of fusible interfacing on bias as shown, and fuse in place, one at a time. Or cut a layer of Pellon fleece and hand catch to the armhole and shoulder seam.

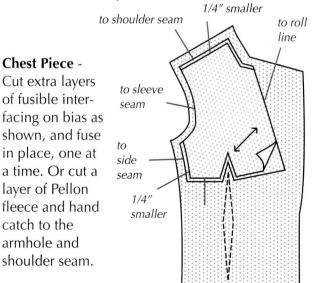

to shoulder seam
1/4" smaller
to roll line
to sleeve seam
to side seam
1/4" smaller

Back - If jacket is unlined, there is a two-piece back stay made of lining fabric. This allows for reaching movement. We prefer a one-piece sew-in back stay in lined men's jackets, just like in women's (page 76).

Sleeves - Elbows seem to be the first place to wear out in most fabrics. Cut an oval of fusible interfacing with pinking shears to camouflage the edges. Center this patch over the elbow area and fuse in place.

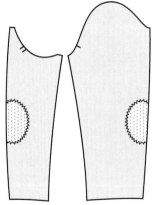
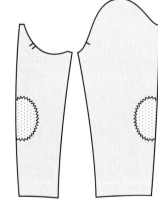

one-piece sleeve   *two-piece sleeve*

Pockets - Use the No-Fail Welt Pocket instructions on page 69-75 for both the inside and outside pockets rather than the instructions from the patterns as this method will generally be easier! Use the "without flap" instructions for the inside pockets and sew as many of them as you want. Most men really appreciate additional inside pockets.

Index

PRODUCTS

These ready-to-use, information-filled sewing how-to books, manuals and videos can be found in local book and fabric stores or ordered through Palmer/Pletsch Publishing (see next page)

LARGE BOOKS

The BUSINE$$ of Teaching Sewing
Second Edition 128 pages, $29.95

Couture—The Art of Fine Sewing
208 pages, $29.95

Creative Serging for the Home and Other Quick Decorating Ideas
160 pages, $19.95

Dream Sewing Spaces— Design and Organization for Spaces Large and Small
128 pages, $19.95

Fit for Real People: Sew Great Clothes Using ANY Pattern
256 pages, $24.95

The Food Nanny Rescues Dinner— Easy Family Meals for Every Day of the Week *288 pages, $24.95*

Hand Mending Made Easy
60 pages, $14.95

Jackets for Real People: Tailoring Made Easy
256 pages, $24.95

Looking Good— A Comprehensive Guide to Wardrobe Planning, Color and Personal Style Development
160 pages, $19.95

Pants for Real People: Fit and Sew for ANY Body
176 pages, $24.95

Sewing Ultrasuede® Brand Fabrics—Ultrasuede®, Ultrasuede Light™, Caress™, Ultraleather™
128 pages, $16.95

Théâtre de la Mode— Fashion Dolls: The Survival of Haute Couture
192 pages, $29.95

These books are all soft-cover. Some larger books are available with coil binding for an additional $5.00.

SMALL BOOKS

Mother Pletsch's Painless Sewing
128 pgs., $9.95

Sewing With Sergers— The Complete Handbook for Overlock Sewing *Revised Edition 128 pages, $9.95*

Creative Serging—The Complete Handbook for Decorative Overlock Sewing
128 pages, $9.95

Pants For Any Body *Fourth Edition*
128 pages, $8.95

The Shade Book *Revised*
140 pages, $11.95

Smart Packing Made Easy
Revised Edition
240 pages, $19.95

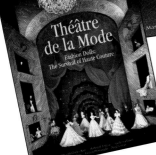

MY FIRST SEWING BOOK KITS

A series of learn-to-sew book kits for children ages 5 and up. Teacher materials also! *Each book, 8½" x 8½", 40 pages*

HAND SEWING
each book alone $10.95
book with kit $14.95

My First Sewing Book

My First Embroidery Book *e-book only, $8.95*

My First Doll Book

MACHINE SEWING
each book alone $10.95
book with kit $12.95

My First Machine Sewing Book

My First Patchwork Book

My First Quilt Book

Teaching Children to Sew Manual and Video,
$29.95 112-page, 8½" x 11"
Additional kit supplies, patterns and teaching materials available.

DVD VIDEOS

Look for these and more Interactive DVDs:

Serger Basics *2 hours $19.95*

Creative Serging *2 hours $19.95*

21st Century Sewing *1 hour $19.95*

Fit for Real People: BASICS *90 minutes $19.95*

Full Busted? Sew Clothes That Fit *2 hours $19.95*

Jackets for Real People *2 hours 45 minutes $24.95*

Learn to Sew and Shirt or Blouse *1 hour $19.95*

Looking Good, Live! *40 minutes $19.95*

Pants for Real People, Fitting Techniques *90 minutes $19.95*

Pants for Real People, Sewing Techniques *90 minutes $19.95*

Perfect Fusing *45 minutes $14.95*

Sew an Ultrasuede® Jacket *1 hour $19.95*

Sewing...Good to Great. It's in the Details *1 hour $19.95*

INTERFACINGS

Our extra-wide fusible weft **PerfectFuse™ Interfacings** are available in four weights. *1-yard and 3-yard packages charcoal black and ecru-white*

Perfect WAISTBANDS™
1" x 5 yds $4.95

PerfectFuse SHEER *$7.95/$23.50*
PerfectFuse LIGHT *$7.95/$23.50*
PerfectFuse MEDIUM *$8.95/$26.50*
PerfectFuse TAILOR*Ultra* *$12.95/$38.50*

Needle Threader for hand & machine needles. *$4.95*

FOR PERFECT SEWING...

Perfect Sew liquid wash-away stabilizer
8.5 oz. spray $11.95
35 oz. refill $24.95

Perfect Pattern Paper
two 84" x 48" sheets $6.95

PALMER/PLETSCH WORKSHOPS

Topics include *Pant Fit, Fit, Tailoring, Creative Serging, Ultrasuede, Couture, Sewing Update, Beginning Sewing and Beginning Quilting Teacher Trainings, Intermediate Sewing,* and *Sewing Camp.* Held at the Palmer/ Pletsch International Training Center in Portland, Oregon.
Teacher training sessions are also available on some topics.

Check your local fabric and book stores for Palmer/Pletsch books and products or contact
Palmer/Pletsch Publishing, 1801 N.W. Upshur Street, Suite 100, Portland, OR 97209
(503) 274-0687 or fax (503) 274-1377 or 1-800-728-3784 (orders) info@palmerpletsch.com

www.palmerpletsch.com